CHASING SPACE

LELAND MELVIN

PRAISE FOR *CHASING SPACE*

"It reminded me of how small the planet really is, and, therefore, of how insignificant our differences as humans are—the kind of issues that kept my own legacy at NASA hidden for so long. *Chasing Space* is a must-read—a flight you should not miss."
—Katherine Johnson, former NASA physicist and mathematician, and recipient of the Presidential Medal of Freedom

"*Chasing Space* reminds us of the value of staying positive and pushing through adversity. It is inspiring and uplifting."
—Simon Sinek, the "Unshakable Optimist" and author of *Start with Why* and *Leaders Eat Last*

"Leland Melvin will take you, too, on a journey."
—Pharrell Williams

"A heartfelt offering for fans of inspiring memoirs, sports lovers, or those interested in the STEM fields."
—*School Library Journal*

"In *Chasing Space*, Leland Melvin tackles stupendous obstacles with dogged determination, showing you what is indeed possible in life—if you believe."
—Neil deGrasse Tyson, Astrophysicist at the American Museum of Natural History and *New York Times* bestselling author of *Welcome to the Universe*

US $6.99 / $8.50 CAN
ISBN 978-0-06-266593-5

harpercollinschildrens.com

9 780062 665935

50699

CHASING
SPACE

YOUNG READERS' EDITION

CHASING SPACE

YOUNG READERS' EDITION

BY LELAND MELVIN

Amistad

An Imprint of HarperCollinsPublishers

Amistad is an imprint of HarperCollins Publishers.

Chasing Space Young Readers' Edition
Copyright © 2017 by Leland Melvin LLC
All rights reserved. Printed in the United States of America.
No part of this book may be used or reproduced in any manner whatsoever without written
permission except in the case of brief quotations embodied in critical articles and reviews.
For information address HarperCollins Children's Books, a division of
HarperCollins Publishers, 195 Broadway, New York, NY 10007.
www.harpercollinschildrens.com

Library of Congress Control Number: 2017934703
ISBN 978-0-06-266592-8 (trade bdg.)
ISBN 978-0-06-266593-5 (pbk.)

19 20 21 22   CG/LSCH   10 9 8 7 6 5 4 3
❖
First Edition

This book is dedicated to my family:
my father, who exemplified grit; my mother, who exudes
her namesake, Grace; my sister, who shows me love;
and my niece, Second Chances.
And finally, my great-niece, who inspires my childlike
wonder, infused with hope and optimism.
Thank you, Mom, Dad, Cat, Britt, and C.

Love, Leland

CHAPTER 1
I REALLY CAN'T HEAR

This was it—April 3, 2001. My first day of spacewalk training. Like all astronauts, I couldn't wait to leave Planet Earth and soar into space. But first I had to learn how to walk in space. Not easy, especially while you're traveling 17,500 miles an hour, 249 miles above Earth. That's like learning to walk while speeding around the planet more than thirty times faster than your average jet travels and being on top of a Mount Everest that's forty-five times bigger than the actual Mount Everest.

Like I said, not easy.

But mastering the technical skills for spacewalking

is the fastest way for an astronaut to get a NASA flight assignment. Just because you're an astronaut doesn't mean you ever get to go into space. To go into space, you need to get assigned to a flight. It's the last step in a journey that can take a lifetime. And not all astronauts walk in space. Some command or pilot the spacecraft. Others are mission specialists who do scientific experiments or work the shuttle's robotic arm. But astronauts who are trained in spacewalking are always in demand. More than anything, I wanted a flight assignment and was willing to do whatever it would take to get one.

Astronauts do their spacewalk training—also known as extravehicular activity (EVA) training—in a 40-foot-deep pool of water. A space shuttle and a replica of the International Space Station are submerged at the bottom of the pool, and the EVA suits we wear, combined with the water, make us feel like we are in the weightless environment of space. The white, puffy suits we wear underwater are almost identical to the ones astronauts wear when we're out in the stratosphere. The only difference is that the underwater suits have extra material that provides more buoyancy to better simulate the weightless feeling of being in space.

When my turn came to train, I put on my equipment and began my descent into the water, ready to master the tasks in front of me as quickly as possible. I wanted to show

NASA that I could do everything from attaching hardware to the outside of the space station to walking by pulling myself along with my hands instead of using my feet.

When astronauts prepare for a spacewalk, we spend eight hours practicing in the pool for every one hour we'll be working in space. The reason we spend so much time training is to make sure that we prepare for anything and everything that could go wrong.

On that fateful April day, I had reached a depth of about ten feet when I noticed that a little block of Styrofoam, called a Valsalva Pad, was missing. The pad is standard equipment in our EVA helmets. It is used to help a diver clear his ears and adapt to increasing air pressure while underwater. We need it because our ears can't always keep up with the changes in pressure that come when we're descending into the pool. It can be hard to hear. Sometimes it can hurt a little, until we "pop" our ears by yawning, swallowing, or by using the pad. To clear your ears with the Valsava Pad, you press your nose against the pad to block your nostrils and then close your mouth and blow out your nose. But my suit didn't have a pad. For whatever reason, that small but very important piece was missing.

As soon as I noticed the missing pad, I used my headset to let test director Greg Sims know. He suggested I come out of the pool to have one installed, but I knew that any delay in my training exercises would lead to a delay in my being assigned a mission. I told Greg I'd stick it out.

"Okay," he said. "Just don't hurt yourself."

Greg is a good friend and great test director. He's dedicated his life to helping astronauts prepare for space travel. He's also a huge football fan. He couldn't believe that I had once played for his favorite team, the Dallas Cowboys. Maybe that's why he agreed to let me stay in the pool. Either way, at the time we were both convinced that it wasn't going to be a problem.

And boy were we wrong.

Before long, my ears felt full. I tried to clear them by pressing my nose up against the helmet neck ring, but it was too far away.

Doctors later said that my high tolerance for pain and my background as a pro athlete probably kept me from realizing how serious the problem had become. I was used to playing through pain. Part of me always thought if it doesn't hurt, it doesn't work.

But by the time I was about twenty feet below the surface, I knew something was really wrong. "I can't hear," I told Greg. "Can you turn the volume up?"

I strained to make out a response, but all I heard was static. I thought something was wrong with my headset or with the cable running from my suit to the pool deck. Maybe a kink in the cable had shut down the communication system. I assumed they were working to fix the problem, but under the water, it felt like they were ignoring me.

"Turn up the volume," I shouted into the microphone.

Instead of doing that, they raised me slowly up and then lowered me down in the water again. They did that a few times, but I still couldn't hear Greg. Seconds later, more crackles and static came over the headset. There was a voice underneath the noise, but it wasn't clear. I couldn't make out the words.

"I really can't hear you," I said.

Minutes later, I was being pulled to the pool's surface.

Far below, my fellow trainee Danny Olivas was at the bottom of the pool, ready to prove his mastery of the EVA tasks. I knew he was probably wondering if my problem was going to slow him down.

Dr. Richard McCluskey, the NASA flight surgeon, was poolside when I came out of the water. I saw his mouth moving, but I couldn't hear anything he said. I couldn't understand why he didn't just speak up. I kept telling him to speak up. Everyone around me looked concerned. They were all moving their mouths, but I couldn't make out what they were saying. It was like watching a movie with the mute button on.

The doctor reached out and touched my right ear. I saw blood on his finger. It was running down my face. Until that moment, I still thought the problem had been with my headset. Suddenly, I knew it was something else. Even so, I didn't think there was a major problem. I trusted the flight surgeons. NASA was like a family to me. These were the best doctors in the world. This was a minor setback. They'd fix whatever was wrong.

Standing by the side of the training pool, Dr. McCluskey looked into my ears and saw that my eardrums were pushed farther back inside my ears than they should have been. He thought the change in underwater pressure had caused it, so he gave me a nasal spray and then blew air into my nose to inflate the middle ear.

My ears were still blocked.

Then he decided to walk me around the corner to the hypobaric altitude chamber, which makes you feel like you're going up in an airplane. He thought another change in air pressure might help clear my ears.

The chamber was a steel tube able to simulate being at an altitude of 10,000 feet. The Empire State Building is 1,250 feet tall—so being in the chamber felt like being on top of eight Empire State Buildings stacked one on top of another! At first I didn't feel any different, but when Dr. McCluskey blew air into my nose again, my ears cleared and I could hear a little better. I could hear people talking from about five feet away. But the minute they adjusted the settings so that it felt like I was back at sea level, my ears blocked up. I couldn't hear, again.

While I was sitting in the chamber, waiting for them to figure out what to do next, everything started to spin. They took me to the showers, where the spinning got the better of me and I threw up.

From there I was taken to the Flight Medicine Clinic and then to Houston Methodist Hospital. Dr. Bobby Alford, an ear, nose, and throat specialist, gave me a battery of hearing and balance tests. I had severe hearing loss in both ears. Dr. Alford recommended we act as soon as possible to diagnose and resolve the problem.

Just a few hours before, I had been on top of the world. I was confident that I would soon be doing what only a handful of people had ever done before—performing spacewalks hundreds of miles above Earth. Now I was deaf and getting ready for exploratory surgery.

I woke up in the recovery room. Dr. Alford let me know what was going on by scribbling on a yellow legal pad. The severe change in underwater pressure had damaged my ears in some way, but the surgery hadn't revealed exactly what went wrong, and you can't fix a problem you can't identify.

My sudden deafness was a medical mystery.

That was heartbreaking news, but I was even more worried about what NASA would say. If we didn't find the cause of my hearing loss and a way to fix it, NASA wouldn't let me fly. My status was about to be changed to "DNIF," or Duty Not Involving Flying.

In my life, I've had my fair share of disappointments. But somehow every failure and every setback has led me to another opportunity. But this time felt different. This time, this setback, the shock of it, the blood dripping out of my ear, the looks on everyone's faces . . . it felt permanent. Lying in a hospital room bed in Houston, I couldn't help but fear that I'd have to give up being an astronaut and exploring space.

And if I didn't have that dream to chase, what did I have at all?

CHAPTER 2
FAMILY, FAITH, AND COMMUNITY

A lot of people assume that I always wanted to be an astronaut or a football player. But they're wrong. When I was growing up, I wanted to be a great tennis player. Like Arthur Ashe.

When I was growing up, Arthur Ashe was a legend. He was the first black man to win major tennis tournaments like the US Open, the Australian Open, and Wimbledon. On the court, he was a model of concentration and grace. I still say he had the best one-handed backhand of anyone who ever played tennis. But Arthur Ashe was more than just a great athlete. He was also a gifted author, a scholar, and an activist.

When I was born in 1964, my parents, Deems and Gracie Melvin, took me home to an apartment owned by Dr. Robert Walter "Whirlwind" Johnson, a tennis coach and physician, in Lynchburg, Virginia. Later we moved to Pierce Street, where Arthur Ashe had spent a few summers beginning in 1953 to train with Dr. Johnson.

Dr. Johnson, who also coached tennis great Althea Gibson, helped break down the color barriers in tennis. At a time when African-Americans were not allowed to play on public tennis courts because of their race, Johnson opened his personal court and founded a tennis camp for black children. He was also the first black doctor to be allowed to practice medicine in Lynchburg's hospitals. Before then, African-American doctors and patients had to go to what were known as "colored" hospitals.

Dr. Johnson taught Ashe to be a gentleman as well as a champion. Ashe's faultless behavior off the courts earned him the respect of millions of fans, including my dad. Arthur Ashe had once been a skinny black kid, just like me. And I wanted to be just like him.

Arthur Ashe wasn't the only African-American hero to visit my neighborhood on Pierce Street. Anne Spencer, an important black poet, lived just a few blocks from Dr. Johnson. Spencer was a force in the civil rights movement. Scientists like George Washington Carver, who pioneered research into peanuts and sweet potatoes as alternative crops to cotton; scholars like Thurgood Marshall, who became the first African-American Supreme Court Justice; and even civil rights leader Dr. Martin Luther King Jr. visited her home. The Lynchburg chapter of the National Association for the Advancement of Colored People (NAACP), a civil rights organization that continues to fight for equality today, was founded in her living room.

Anne's son Chauncey was a civil rights activist like his mother. Chauncey wanted to be a pilot, but in the 1920s, no one in the South would give a black man flying lessons. So Chauncey moved to Chicago, where he was able to learn to fly. In 1936 he and another black pilot, Dale Lawrence White, flew a rented plane on a ten-city tour that started in Chicago and ended in Washington, DC. The flight got a lot of attention, especially in the black press, and convinced Congress to include blacks in the Civilian Pilot Training Program. That led to the establishment of World War II's Tuskegee Airmen. The success and bravery of those military fighter pilots opened up aviation opportunities for all African-Americans, including me.

I didn't know it when I was a child, but these Pierce Street legends cleared the path for my success and the success of many others. They changed the course of history. And I think of them often. Their daring and skill made possible the opportunities that were available to me. Because of them, the skies are open to anyone with the grit and determination to explore the unknown and advance our knowledge of the universe.

FROM PIERCE STREET TO HILLTOP DRIVE

Before I started elementary school, my parents decided to buy their first home. We moved to Hilltop Drive, across from Fire Station Number 3 in the Fort Hill area of Lynchburg. It was a neighborhood with backyards and lots of space to run around and play. It was also a place where the neighbors looked out for one another.

A few months after I was born, the Civil Rights Act of 1964 was passed. That law made it illegal to discriminate against people based on race, religion, or their sex. Up until then, much of the South was segregated—blacks and whites lived in different neighborhoods and went to different schools. Some businesses refused service to black customers. Blacks had to drink out of separate water fountains and ride in the back of the bus.

I never had to experience that kind of segregation. Our Hilltop Drive neighborhood was about 40 percent black and 60 percent white, and we all got along. My school was integrated, and I played with white kids as well as black kids.

At the time, Lynchburg made sure that schools were integrated by busing students from one neighborhood school to another. Some kids wound up going to schools across town, but my older sister, Cathy, and I were lucky enough to get to stay in our neighborhood school until I was bused to Dunbar Middle School, which was across town.

My parents both taught at Linkhorne Middle School. They were well known in the neighborhood and respected throughout town. I look back proudly on the fact that my parents were educators, but at the time, it meant my sister and I never got away with anything!

When I was in Mrs. Martin's fourth-grade class, Brandon Miller and I were fooling around and knocked over a desk. Mrs. Martin wasn't happy, and that meant a visit to the principal's office. Back then kids got paddled for misbehaving in school, and Mrs. Carwile, the principal, did her job.

But that wasn't the end of it.

My best friend was a kid named Butch Jones, and Butch's mother was a teacher in the Lynchburg City Schools. She heard about my getting into trouble before Butch did, and when I went over to his house that afternoon after school, his mother was waiting.

"Leland, come over here," his mom said calmly from the kitchen.

When I got there, she sat me down and let me have it. "What in the world were you thinking, behaving like that in school? You know better."

That scolding hurt more than the paddling. But that still wasn't the end of it!

Mrs. Carwile called my home that evening, as I knew she would. A few minutes later, I heard my dad's footsteps on the stairs. I knew he'd have a switch in his hand and I'd get another spanking.

It might seem like a lot of fuss for overturning a desk. But even then I knew that all of those people were looking out for me. They wanted me to do and be my best. They wanted me to understand right and wrong. I might not have appreciated the lesson at the time, but I never doubted that they were looking out for my best interests.

My parents were always a unified team. If I was in trouble with one of them, I was in trouble with both of them. I don't remember my parents ever pressuring me to get good grades. They expected me to be good and to work hard like they expected me to wash behind my ears and finish the food on my plate. It was something they did not have to tell me to do. I just knew. They didn't check my homework. They didn't force me to study. I did my homework and prepared for my exams because I knew it was expected of me. Because I always wanted to do my best and I always wanted to make them proud.

My parents also expected me to learn outside of school, too. When I was about eight years old, they bought me a chemistry set. One afternoon I was experimenting with different chemical solutions, mixing them together to see what could happen. And kaboom! I set off an explosion that burned a nice-sized hole in the carpet.

My mother rushed into the room, expecting to find me blown to bits, but I was sitting on the couch with a big smile on my face. I'm sure I got in trouble—and I'm sure that chemistry set eventually was taken off the store shelves. But more than anything, I remember realizing in that moment that I was going to become a scientist. I wanted to learn everything about how the world worked. For the school science fair that year, I used my new chemistry skills and made a volcano. Watching it erupt and seeing the lava pour down the sides was the best part of the project. Knowing that I knew how to make that happen thrilled me to no end.

My mother loved to read, and she passed her passion along to my sister and me. She read to us every night when we were young. Early favorites included stories like *The Little Engine That Could* and *Curious George*. Curiosity and the "I think I can, I think I can" refrain from *The Little Engine* inspired me in a million different ways. When the going gets tough, I still come back to those lessons. They remind me to never stop experimenting and to never stop trying.

Young people often ask me who my heroes are, and my first answer is always "my father." I learned so many lessons from him. One of the most lasting was the importance of vision. My father would visualize a goal and work toward it tirelessly. He taught me to see past the obstacles in front of me and to always believe in myself.

One morning when I was about eleven, he drove up to the house in a bread truck.

"What's that for?" I asked.

"It's going to be our camper," he said.

A camper? I thought. It was a bread truck! How could our whole family sleep in it? There was only one seat for the driver with just one big open space and no place for beds. But my father had a vision, and like it or not, I was enlisted into the project.

Over the next few weeks we installed bunk beds that folded up against the wall, and a pullout couch. Suddenly a truck with no beds now had four. We added a camping stove and a small table to create a kitchen area. We bolted everything to the floor or the walls—not an easy job! It wasn't fancy, but it had everything we needed. We traveled all over the country in that old bread truck, from the Smoky Mountains of North Carolina to the Appalachian Mountains and all the way south to Disney World in Florida.

Turning that bread truck into a camper taught me an important lesson: Everything starts with a vision. You can't create something great if you can't "see" what that great thing is from the start.

That said, sometimes pushing your kids to solve problems creatively can have some pretty funny, unintended consequences. I remember one night when my mother wouldn't let Cathy and me leave the dinner table because we hadn't finished our dinners.

"When I come back," she said, "I don't want to see any food left on those plates."

Cathy was sitting next to an open window. My sister reasoned that my mother hadn't ordered us to *eat* the food. She only said that our plates needed to be clean. So, the offending vegetables and meat went out the window, and when my mother returned, we presented her with our clean plates.

I can't imagine we got away with it. Eventually, my mother must have discovered a pile of food in the yard. I don't remember our punishment, only my sister's creative solution to our problem.

When I was in middle school, some of the neighborhood kids started skateboarding on our street. That looked like fun to me, and so I asked my dad for a skateboard. We didn't have money for a lot of extras, so my father told me that if I wanted a skateboard, I had to build one myself.

Well, I'd never built a skateboard before, but knew exactly what I wanted. I had my "vision." I got a piece of wood from the Dunbar Middle School's wood shop and shaped it into a base. I had a newspaper route by then, and I saved up my earnings to buy wheels. Like the bread truck, it wasn't perfect, but it worked. I had the skateboard I wanted and I learned that I could build something from nothing. I was proud of my work, and I had a lot of fun racing around my neighborhood on my one-of-a-kind skateboard.

Building the skateboard gave me a shot of confidence, and so my next project was to make a bicycle out of spare parts. I had learned how well-built things should fit together. I had learned how to imagine what I wanted to make, what I wanted as the final result. So I took all that I'd learned, and through a lot of trial and error, I figured out how to build myself a bicycle. It probably should come as no surprise, then, that when our telephone broke, I decided to fix it myself. I took the phone apart and reconstructed it by attaching the pieces to a wood board. By the time I finished, the only thing that looked like a telephone was the handset, but it worked! There's no better way to learn, I think, than by learning with your own two hands. And doing these things on my own was what put me on my path to becoming an engineer.

FAITH AND COMMUNITY

My parents had a strong vision for our family, for the kind of people Cathy and I would grow up to be. That vision extended to our community, too.

My father taught language arts at Linkhorne Middle School. His students loved and trusted him. I'd come home from school and find him sitting with his students, going over papers or offering guidance or just listening to what they had to say. First and foremost, my father always treated everyone with respect and kindness.

Teenagers with difficult home lives often ended up at our house. They knew my parents' door was always open, even when others in the neighborhood didn't want them around. Stan Hull, a teammate on my high school football team, once told me: "I knew I was always welcome in Mr. Melvin's house. He saw promise in everyone."

Robert Flood was another local guy who put his trust in my dad. Robert lived with his grandmother and started getting into trouble in middle school. He was a great athlete, but he caused a lot of problems in class. He wound up getting expelled in high school, which cost him a chance to play college basketball.

When his grandmother died, Robert thought he had no one. It didn't take long for him to get in serious trouble. Robert was arrested and sent to jail, but even then my father refused to abandon him. "He took the time," Robert said. "He listened, and he treated me like I was his son."

Robert's life had many ups and downs. He battled a drug addiction that very nearly ruined him. But when he walked out of a treatment center ready for a fresh start, my father was there waiting. He found Robert a job and knew he needed a car, so my father found him one—on the strict condition that Robert stay employed and out of trouble.

And he did. Robert eventually went back to school and got a college degree. Years later, when he spoke at my father's funeral, Robert said he felt like he'd lost his own dad.

Robert's was just one of many lives my father touched. My father had a passion for the gospel. He believed that he was put on Earth to serve others. He also played drums, keyboard, and trumpet in a gospel band. If you caught them on the right night, you would hear that he was a great singer, too.

My father and his band often set up next to the downtown neighborhood basketball court. They'd cook up hot dogs and hamburgers for whoever came by. Boys would come to play hoops, but they'd always stop and eat and listen to my father preach and play gospel music first.

My mother was also deeply involved in our church and in the community. She taught home economics at Linkhorne. Her students learned to sew and cook. She taught them etiquette, too, which was an invaluable skill to have in the South in the 1970s. For many of the girls she taught, my mother was the only adult they trusted.

My parents' vision for our family and our future came

from their limitless Christian faith. And I would never have made it to space without constantly calling on that faith myself.

Faith and school—these were two mainstays of life in the Melvin family. But for me growing up, there was a third thing that mattered almost as much as the first two—and that was sports.

CHAPTER 3
BECOMING AN ATHLETE

I loved sports. Whether I was just running around on a playground with my friends or pitching fastballs or playing center field for my Little League team, sports were always a big part of my life.

When I was in elementary school, I would stop at my good friend Sam Hughes's house every morning before school to play basketball. Our school was about a mile from his house, so we'd play until ten minutes before the bell was due to ring. We'd stop, no matter who was winning, and sprint to school. That might be one of the reasons why I was such a fast runner!

I started playing football in elementary school. We had to supply our own equipment, and because money was tight, my father had to borrow what I needed from a middle school in town. My pants, pads, and jersey were all a little too big, but it was the helmet I remember most. It also was a bit too big, and had definitely seen better days. We cleaned it up the best we could, but there was a smell that just wouldn't go away. I wore that smelly helmet for the entire football season.

I remember the day everyone on the team met on the field to paint our helmets and stencil a *P* for Perrymont Elementary School Panthers on the side. In that line of helmets waiting to be painted, mine stood out. There was some teasing about my old, smelly helmet, but I didn't let it bother me. Once the helmets were painted, they all looked the same. And the teasing only made me more determined to show them what I could do on the field.

My dad recognized how important sports were to me and how they could be a path to achieving my goals. Sports taught me to stay focused and be disciplined. My dad coached my Little League baseball team, and he even talked the Lynchburg Recreation Department into building a public park and a basketball court up the hill from our house. The Fort Avenue Park became the place to go on Sundays after church. The small park was filled with so many ballers that if you lost your first game you couldn't play for the rest of the day. I played any time I could get into a game—against kids my own age, high schoolers, and even grown men.

In high school, I became a wide receiver on the football team. But when the football season wrapped up, I moved right on to basketball and then tennis. I loved all three sports, though, honestly, tennis was my favorite then and now. Between studies and my teams, I didn't have a lot of free time, but I had a posse of five friends. We called ourselves the Big Blue Crew, and whenever we had a minute of free time, we got together. There was Philip Scott, nicknamed "Silky Blue" because he had a smooth-sounding voice and could talk his way out of just about anything. Bryant "Boogie Bear" Anderson was always dancing, and Ernest "Gus" Hawkins was always talking about his favorite basketball player, Gus Johnson. Ernest Penn had two nicknames, one from his family ("FuFu") but we also called him "Moon" after a character in a movie we had seen together. The guys called my father "Big D," for Deems, so naturally I became "Little D" for Little Deems, as I was his mini-me.

When we were acting up at my house, my father used to say, "Don't make me get that right shoe," meaning that he would give us a swat with it. That turned into a catchphrase the Big Blue Crew used on one another, when one of us was giving the others a hard time. We would tease, "Don't make me get that right shoe!"

We had lots of fun together—in school, on playgrounds, and on more formal teams. FuFu was a quarterback on the high school football team, and Boogie Bear was our running back. All five of us were on the basketball team.

The football coaches at Heritage High School, Mark Storm and Jimmy Green, focused on building strong character as well as strong athletes. But the coach who made the biggest difference was Rufus Knight.

Coach Knight joined the staff of Heritage High as our offensive coordinator in 1976. He was a deeply religious man who, like my father, lived his faith every day. If you played on Coach Knight's team, he took care of you. That included driving all over Lynchburg to drop off players after a game or a late practice. He always made sure his players were safely inside before driving on to the next house.

It was Coach Knight and Coach Green who gave me the second chance that would change everything for me. It was the first of many second chances that turned my life around.

It was the senior year homecoming game against our rivals, the Rustburg Red Devils. It had been a long, intense game. The score was tied, with only minutes left. College scouts were in the audience looking for talent, but I didn't think they were there for me. I intended to go to UVA or Virginia Tech to study engineering. Playing college ball wasn't on my radar.

But I really wanted to win this game for the alumni who had supported the team and who had come to town just for the homecoming game. The crowd was alive and loud. It was hard to hear the plays being called, but with hand signals and lots of yelling and staring, we somehow found a way to communicate.

I remember the score was tied 14–14 and there was just a minute or two left in the game. Stan Hull, our starting quarterback, called a nine route. That meant I would have to run as fast and as far as I could toward the end zone while Stan threw a Hail Mary pass my way. I flanked out wide on the 50-yard line, looked at the defender, and then looked back at the ball. It was too loud to hear Stan, so I had to watch the second the ball was snapped. I exploded off the line of scrimmage. The defender tried to jam me, but I countered and rushed past him. In my periphery, I saw the fans on their feet as Stan launched a tight, perfect spiral that was on a trajectory to meet me in the end zone.

I adjusted my speed and raised my hands to catch the victory pass. I had done this a thousand times in practice.

Then the unthinkable happened. I dropped the ball. The most important pass of my entire high school career, and I dropped it.

I looked into the stands and saw people shaking their

heads in disbelief. I didn't know it at the time, but Morgan Hout, a scout from the University of Richmond, was standing near the end zone. When he saw me drop the pass, he turned and headed for the exit.

I expected to be benched for the final play of the game. But that's not what happened. Coach Green and Coach Knight had already discussed the next play when I trudged to the sideline. Coach Green grabbed me by the face mask, looked me in the eyes, and said, "Get back out there, run the same play, and catch the ball."

I would have let that single botched play define my high school career, but they gave me a second chance. Honestly, if they hadn't sent me back out there, dropping that pass would have changed my whole life. My coaches believed in me more than I believed in myself. They weren't going to let me leave the field on a mistake.

"You had worked so hard," Coach Knight said to me years later. "We just believed in you."

I went back to the huddle and delivered the same play to my teammates. They were angry. I had just let them down, and now I was being given the opportunity to let them down again.

"We all wondered why, if it didn't work the first time, would it work the second?" Stan remembered.

But there was no time for an argument. We were a team, and the coaches had given us the play. We broke the huddle, lined up on the ball, and on the snap I took off for the end zone again. Stan threw another perfect spiral to the same exact spot, and this time I caught it for the touchdown. The crowd erupted with the loudest, happiest cheers I had ever heard.

Hout heard the cheers erupt in the stadium, turned around, and walked back toward the end zone. I was celebrating the victory with my teammates, the ball in my hand. Not only had we won the game, but that catch led to a full football scholarship at the University of Richmond, worth $180,000.

That one chance changed the whole course of my life. That night, my coaches' belief in me, their willingness to give me a second chance, inspired me. I was not going to let them down then—or ever. Their faith continues to inspire me to persevere against the odds. I take it as a point of pride that I never give up. Not then, not now, not ever.

I wish I could say that after that homecoming catch, the rest of high school went smoothly. But it didn't. Heritage High was a large and integrated school. The students got along pretty well, but every now and then the limits were tested. Some people didn't approve of kids of different races spending time together.

In the 1970s, racism in Lynchburg was alive and well. There was the casual day-to-day racism of the women who'd clutch their purses tighter when they saw me, a black boy, coming up the street, or people who would use the "n-word" in my presence. In middle school, I worked part-time as a janitor for my neighbor, Mr. Davis, who had his own cleaning company. Once I was cleaning the men's bathroom in one of the big banks downtown when the bank president came in. I greeted him politely. Instead of answering, the man looked at me as if I were an alien and left the room. Whether it was because I was a janitor or because I was black, I'll never know for sure, but I'll never forget the bad feeling that he left me with. I learned to be alert and attentive to other people in sensitive situations. I realized that I never wanted to make anyone feel the way he made me feel. It was a lesson in empathy for me, one that I carry with me to this day.

Even worse, though, was an encounter I had with a Virginia state trooper on the night of my high school graduation. I was dating a smart, pretty girl who also happened to be of a different race. She had just been accepted to the University of Virginia. On graduation night we were talking in my car when a state trooper quietly drove up behind us with his lights off. We knew enough to immediately be worried. Though I'd always found Lynchburg to be a diverse and accepting place, I knew there still were cops from outside our community who didn't appreciate people of different races dating.

He pointed his flashlight into the passenger window

and told my girlfriend to roll down the window.

"Young lady, please get out of the car and join me in the patrol car," the officer said. He was white and a big guy. The uniform he wore and the gun in his holster made him look even bigger.

My girlfriend had no choice but to get out and move into the front seat of the patrol car.

"Who is that you're with? What are y'all doing?" the officer demanded. "If you don't tell me, I'm going to take you both down to the jail, where your parents will have to pick you up."

I knew he wanted to scare my girlfriend into telling him that I had somehow tricked her or forced her into my car. That was how it worked for some people back then. This particular state trooper clearly wanted the chance to teach me a lesson, but my girlfriend didn't fall for it.

"That's my boyfriend. He's a good guy," she said. "We just graduated. We're about to go to college. He's got a full scholarship."

The officer wanted her to change her story. He kept barking at her, trying to get her to say that I had forced her into my car. "He assaulted you, didn't he?" the officer said. "He forced himself on you."

Each time she said no, he said he'd take us both down to the police station and call our parents. He thought that would embarrass her into changing her story, but she refused.

The next thing I knew, I was sitting in the back of the patrol car, while he tried to bully me, too. He wasn't outright disrespectful, but he was commanding—someone who was used to getting his way. And he was trying to get me to say I had done something wrong, when I hadn't.

Surrounded by flashing red-and-blue lights, I became vividly aware of how quickly I could lose everything. That state trooper could have changed the course of my entire life just because he felt like making a point. Going to Lynchburg City Jail on a fake charge would have meant kissing my scholarship good-bye. And if he could have made the charge stand up, I would have had a criminal record and would miss out on college completely.

Stuff like that happens to young black men all over the country. And once a guy ends up with a rap sheet, everything gets exponentially harder. From getting a job to getting a loan to just the way your friends and family treat you. Getting pulled into the legal system on even the flimsiest charges can ruin even the brightest future.

That night, the officer seemed determined to add me to a growing number of young men in prison, but for some reason he changed his mind. "I could have taken you to jail," he told me, "but I'm going to do you both a favor tonight. Get outta here. Don't park here again."

Sometimes life is like that. It's hard to call it being lucky, but it does affirm my faith that someone up there has a plan for me. I ended my high school career all too aware of how easily everything could slip away. After that night, I was all the more determined to make my college years a success.

CHAPTER 4
SECOND CHANCES

My first night at the University of Richmond had me staring into a plastic cup filled with tobacco-laced spit, Tabasco sauce, and other gross ingredients. The football team watched as a 300-pound offensive tackle took on the job of tormenting the new guys with a joy that was more than a little scary.

He twirled his massive arm above our heads with a command. "Drink!"

I choked it down.

Welcome to college football, I thought.

I hoped that would be the end of the hazing, but the

next thing I knew I was tied back-to-back with Taylor Lackey, a defensive back I'd met just a few hours before. The two of us were thrown, blindfolded, into the bed of defensive back Billy Cole's pickup truck and driven around for what felt like hours.

When the truck finally stopped, the players yanked us out of the bed, tossed us onto train tracks, and sped away laughing. The next thing we heard was a train whistle. It got louder and louder as Taylor and I struggled to escape. We managed to roll off the tracks at what felt like the last possible instant. We never did feel the train pass, but I chalked that up to adrenaline and abject terror. A few days later I found out that the train whistle was really an air horn attached to Billy's pickup.

We had succeeded in not getting flattened by a train, but now we had to find a way to get out of our blindfolds, untie ourselves, and make our way back to campus.

The night was dark, and we had been driven around for a long time. My heart was beating fast and my stomach was still churning from my Tabasco-and-spit cocktail.

"Where are we?" Taylor yelled into the night.

Taylor would soon prove himself to be a standout safety and fierce hitter on the football field, but that night we both felt helpless. Large clouds had rolled in so we didn't even have stars to help us navigate. We started walking and soon saw the lights of the library. Billy hadn't taken us far from campus after all. We realized he must have just been driving around in circles.

Taylor and I made it back to our rooms only to be roused out of bed again shortly after for more general harassment. We didn't get much sleep that night.

At practice the next morning we all suited up like nothing had happened. Under the hot July sun, Coach Dal Shealy laid out his strategy for building a winning team. I don't think I heard a single word. My head was pounding too loudly.

I'd like to say that was the end of the hazing, but on my second night in training camp, the veteran players led the freshmen to the big communal bathroom and shaved our heads! I didn't have a lot of hair to start with, so I didn't put up a fight. Don Miller, a big linebacker with a nice, full head of hair, refused to open his bedroom door. "I'm not going to do it!" he yelled.

The upperclassmen warned him that he'd regret it if he didn't come out, but Don wasn't swayed. His room was on the second floor, and he decided to jump out the window to save his hair. Miraculously, he didn't hurt himself, but a few hours later when he tried to creep back into the building, he was ambushed. Don lost his hair just like the rest of us.

I don't defend hazing. It can get out of hand and kids can get hurt. There's an awfully thin line between team-building and plain old bullying. If you're ever in a situation where you're uncomfortable or people are pressuring you to do something that you don't want to do, even if you feel it might disappoint your friends or teammates, you should always walk away and tell an adult. Hazing isn't cool. But teammates do bond by going through shared adversity off the field, and that can bring a team together as much as what happens on the field. No, I would never recommend tying freshmen together and dumping them on the train tracks. Even though it turned out fine, it was a dangerous and silly thing to do. But as a consequence, Taylor and I did become lifelong friends, and we learned that night that we could rely on each other through anything.

The hazing was one thing, but Coach Shealy's training was something else entirely. Even though we were all well-conditioned young athletes, nothing prepared us for the grueling workouts he put us through. He never cut us any slack. He wanted us to be our best, and he pushed the team to the brink of physical and mental exhaustion.

Nobody wanted to disappoint Coach Shealy. He saw coaching as his God-given mission in life. He specifically recruited players who might not have been top athletes but who had the character and determination to be a part of his team. Our behavior off the field was as important to him as our performance on the field.

"My philosophy was to coach the way I like to be

coached," he told me years after I'd graduated. "I wanted to teach my players how to be men, to teach you to live life fully and to be the person you should be."

We may not have won every game, but Coach Shealy got the best out of us, and he made us all better people while doing it.

OUR LOSING SEASON

The University of Richmond had an NCAA football team for more than a century before I got there. But by my freshman year, in September 1982, the program was in serious trouble. In the previous six seasons, the Spiders lost forty-six games, and won only twenty. There was talk of killing the football program. It didn't help that the stadium the team had played in since 1929 was three miles from campus. That made it hard to keep students interested, especially when the team was losing. To make matters worse, the NCAA had just dropped the team down from the Division 1-A to 1-AA, which meant we'd be playing less prestigious schools and weaker teams.

The program was under pressure to turn the losing streak around, and summer training camp was intense. When classes started that fall, I was overwhelmed by my course load and the relentless schedule of training and practices. If I managed to get five hours of sleep, I considered that a good night.

I was still interested in becoming a scientist and had decided to major in chemistry. Lynchburg was in need of good black doctors to carry on Dr. Johnson's legacy, and my parents wanted me to consider going on to medical school. A chemistry major seemed a good first step toward that goal.

My freshman year the Spiders lost every single football game. We ended the season 0–10. Worse, we were demonized around campus. Complete strangers snarled at me. When you're on an athletic scholarship and your team is losing, school administrators, fellow students, and even professors make you feel like you've let them down. Many of them saw me as nothing more than a dumb jock and didn't think I deserved to be there academically.

A few days before classes started, I was in a meeting with my freshman adviser, Dr. J. Ellis Bell, and about twenty other students. Dr. Bell asked for a show of hands from those who were exempt from taking certain classes because of their advanced placement test scores.

"Like Leland here," he said. "He's exempt from taking calculus."

I could feel the surprise from the other students in the room. *Seriously? Him? The black football player?* Their stares made me feel like I had something to prove—off the football field as well as on it.

That first semester was a challenge. Juggling football

and my studies was much more difficult than it had been in high school. But I worked hard, made friends, and believed I was doing well in my classes. Still, I was relieved when final exams were over and it was time to go home for winter break.

It was great returning home to my family. Win or lose in football, they were proud of me. My parents had driven to every single game and I spoke to them all the time, but it was still nice to see them at home. Hot chocolate, a warm fire, and the scent of pine in our house on Hilltop Drive made me forget the losing season. Honestly, I was exhausted. It had been a tough first semester of training, game travel, classes, and finals.

My hardest class that fall had been inorganic chemistry. I'd had a decent grade in the course all semester, so I wasn't too worried about my final grade. Dr. William Myers, the professor, later said that I wasn't his strongest student that year, but I was the most determined. He saw that I had the potential to become a scientist and wanted to help me achieve that.

When my grades came in around Christmastime, there was an X next to inorganic chemistry instead of the A or B I expected. I thought Dr. Myers must have been late getting grades in, even though he had been quick to grade tests during the semester. I didn't see any reason to worry.

HONOR COUNCIL

I returned to school after a few relaxing weeks at home. I came back ready to begin off-season football training and to take on a new set of classes. I was also eager to find out my grade in inorganic chemistry.

I had just dropped off my bags in my dorm when I got a phone call from a senior who was the head of the Richmond College Honor Council. The honor council was a student group that, under the direction of a faculty adviser, examined cases of students who were accused of violating the school's honor code. I figured that he was going to ask me to be a member of the council.

Wow, that's pretty cool, I thought. *And I'm only a freshman.*

I was busy with football and schoolwork, but I thought this would be a good chance to get noticed on campus for something besides the gridiron.

I entered the room and exchanged greetings with two honor council members.

The next words I heard were so shocking that for a moment I thought they were spoken in a foreign language. The council told me I had been accused of cheating in Dr. Myers's Inorganic Chemistry class. Time stopped while I tried to figure out what was going on. The council members looked genuinely concerned, but I could also tell by the looks on their faces that they thought I was guilty.

Tom, a senior who lived across the hall from me in the dorm, was my accuser. He was a business major struggling in what was known as "football chemistry," a basic-level class for non-science majors. During the fall semester, Tom had needed a final grade of B to graduate and had asked me to tutor him. He knew I had a good average in a much more challenging chemistry class. He was also a member of the honor council.

As the honor council related the charge, I remembered the December day in detail. It was almost the end of the semester, and the next day was my chemistry final. Tom had just gotten the result of his final, and we were celebrating his B when his girlfriend walked into the room. A freshman like me, she talked about the inorganic chemistry exam she had just taken under Dr. Myers. It never occurred to me to ask her to stop talking. I didn't need her help with my test, we were in different classes, and my mind was on celebrating Tom's B. But later, Tom reported the two of us for discussing the chemistry exam.

Tom's girlfriend and I both had to stand trial.

I don't remember how much time passed from the day of the accusation to the day I met with the full honor council. It was less than two weeks. I sat across from a dozen or so students, mostly male and all white, whose job it was to judge me. The council was overseen that year by Dr. Richard Mateer, a university dean and, by coincidence, a chemistry professor.

I already stood out on campus. At the time, the number of minority students at the University of Richmond amounted to around 1 percent of the student body—just over 26 in a student body of about 2,600. The fact that the Spiders had lost every game didn't help my case either. It wasn't exactly like I was the big man on campus. At the time, I felt sure no one would have minded all that much if I wasn't still enrolled the next semester.

The trial took about fifteen minutes. I didn't receive any help with my defense; no one from the school's administration ever talked to me or explained my rights. I was alone, facing a panel of students who knew nothing about me but held enormous power over my future. They found me guilty of cheating and suspended me for a semester.

Tom's girlfriend, who sat through a separate trial, received a similar punishment.

After I left the trial I walked to my dorm and sat on the steps, openly crying. I couldn't stomach the thought of having to call my dad and tell him I had been suspended from college. I figured I would lose my scholarship, too.

That day could easily have been my last at the University of Richmond. I sat with my head buried in my hands, shocked and angry. Then my roommate, Dan Fittz, came out and said I had a phone call. Dr. Myers wanted to see me. Dreading what he would say, I dragged myself to his office. I had disappointed him, and I thought he wanted an explanation.

The honor council had recommended to Dr. Myers that he give me a failing grade in his class, but once again, someone handed me a second chance I didn't see coming. Dr. Myers said that I wasn't an F student, but rather, a student who had made a serious mistake.

He knew that a failing grade in the class would change the course of my academic career in ways that might be impossible to reverse. All semester Dr. Myers had been impressed with how I had balanced his very difficult course with my schedule of daily practices and regular game travel. He decided that since I had been willing to work that hard, he would fight for me.

Years later, I contacted Dr. Myers to discuss the cheating accusation. He was reluctant to talk about it. He admitted that he had considered me guilty. I had received advance information about the exam, even if I didn't use it. The question for him, he said, had been what to do about it. I had made a mistake that day by not leaving the room while Tom's girlfriend talked about her test, but he was not going to let that mistake affect the rest of my life.

Dr. Myers was able to override my suspension on the grounds that I complete an ethics course and work in his chemistry lab until I graduated. That punishment turned into a blessing. I still credit those extra hours working in his lab with turning me into a serious scientist.

The following year I took organic chemistry, a notoriously difficult course that is usually the weeding-out for premed students. Years later, my professor, Dr. Stuart Clough, would tell me that he was initially skeptical that I could keep up, but I proved him wrong. I remember him walking through the classroom and dropping a graded test on the desk of each student, facedown. When he got to me, he laid the test on my desk faceup, a B+ written across the top, one of the highest grades that day. "Very good job, Leland," he said. Years later, he recalled that he had been impressed that a football player had done so well.

But what I remember is looking down at the grade in front of me and telling him, "I can do better."

My junior year, I was awarded the department's Merck Index Award for being the Organic Chemistry Student of the Year, and it was Dr. Mateer, the dean in charge of the honor council, who presented me with the award.

More than thirty years later, I returned to the University of Richmond for a Spiders reunion and took a tour of the school's new athletic facilities, including a new meeting room for the football team. I noticed a plaque on the wall. The room was dedicated to me—paid for by the family of the senior who had been head of the honor council back in 1983.

CHAPTER 5
TRAGEDY AND TURNAROUND

Dr. Myers's decision to offer me an alternative punishment instead of suspension didn't win me any friends in some corners of the school, but that didn't bother me. What bothered me was the idea that people believed I had cheated. Once again, I felt like I had something to prove.

I also had to make sure that my friends didn't carry out revenge on my accuser. I'll never know why Tom turned on me the way he did, but my friends and teammates never questioned my honor or my right to be on campus. I was relieved to know that there were people who had my back.

Although football season was over, training continued all year. I had a full load of classes and my job in the lab. That didn't leave me a lot of time for anything else.

In the lab it was often just me, Dr. Myers, and maybe one other student. A football player in the lab was so unusual that during my senior year, *Sports Illustrated* magazine published a photo of me holding a beaker of dry ice while mysterious vapors encircled me.

Under Dr. Myers's guidance, I conducted research on ways to make potentially cancer-curing drugs even more effective. Over the years, my teammates took to calling me "Larry Lab" because the coaches permitted me to show up near the end of practice when training conflicted with my lab work. I took the nickname in good spirits—I've certainly been called worse things—but I held up my end of the bargain on the field every year. The coaches allowed me to make my schoolwork a priority, because they knew they could count on me as a player. I wanted to be part of the team that turned the Spiders' losing streak around, and I was—but that took a while.

The summer after my freshman year I stayed in Richmond to take my first physics course before the fall football season started up again. I was doing research for Dr. Myers and working out in the gym at every opportunity. I was determined that my sophomore year would be different, that we would turn things around and have a winning season.

I couldn't have been more wrong.

Among the standout players my sophomore year was a huge offensive tackle from Marietta, Georgia, named Troy Wirtz. He was six foot six and nearly 300 pounds. The coaches were talking him up as a rising star. He was a good guy and a caring teammate. No one left more of himself on the field than Troy. He wanted to win as badly as anyone I ever played with. That said, there were rumors he was taking steroids, but nobody paid that much attention. This was before the steroids in athletics had such a huge spotlight on them. If you were playing well, people didn't ask a lot of questions.

Four weeks into practice and only two weeks before our first game of the season, Troy drove to the home of his girlfriend in Chester, Virginia. He was furious that she wanted to end their relationship. After an argument, he took out a gun and killed his girlfriend and her mother, wounded her brother, and then shot himself.

The tragedy stunned the university community and the city of Richmond. My teammates and I were distraught. We grieved for Troy and his family as well as his victims. There were rumors that he went nuts from steroids. We didn't understand "roid rage" well back then, but if you were in enough locker rooms, with enough big guys, you knew it happened. Sure, steroids helped build up muscle, but we all knew they came with a lot of risk. Some players couldn't resist, and they took steroids despite the danger. Honestly, I never saw steroids being used, and I certainly never took them. But the truth is that many athletes will be approached by someone who will tell them they have something that will make them stronger, faster, or able to recover more quickly. The allure can be hard to resist. As competitors, we all want to be our best, but the truth is that drugs like steroids do far more harm to your body than they help. Using them is also cheating. It's cheating yourself and your team and your friends and family. There is nothing more satisfying than knowing that you gave it your all on the field—but only when what you gave was yours to give. All I ever wanted was to be my best—and being my best meant playing clean. I never even considered doing it any other way.

Losing one of our best players in such a tragic way set the stage for what would be another challenging year on the field for the Spiders.

Despite the loss of our teammate and the challenges that brought, we did start to turn things around. In October, we snapped what was then the second longest losing streak in college football history by defeating the University of Central Florida 31–26.

The game was tight and UCF was a strong opponent, but late in the game, quarterback Bob Bleier waved me into the end zone and then lofted a perfect pass over the arms of a defender. I was in place to receive the ball for the touchdown.

It was the team's first win since Thanksgiving of 1981. We went on to win two more games that season, finishing 3–8. It was a dramatic improvement over my freshman year—but still our record said we were losers.

THE GROUND SHIFTS

The Spiders' performance on the field changed dramatically during my junior year in 1984. It was as if the ground had shifted; we started to win.

Our first game was against James Madison University. We took control from the start. On the first play after a turnover by JMU, Bleier rolled left and found me wide open. The completion was good for 45 yards and the first Spider touchdown of 1984. I piled up ten receptions for 108 yards in that game, and the University of Richmond newspaper, *The Collegian*, started to refer to Bleier and me as the "B and M Express."

Even more important, the mind-set of the team was transformed from one of disappointment to one of constant improvement and optimism.

Coach Shealy would often tell me, "Leland, close your eyes. You're lined up on the thirty-yard line. You're running a post corner into the end zone. You're accelerating past the defender. You're now looking at the ball. The ball is coming into your hands. You tune out the crowd. You're now in the end zone. You caught the ball. We've won the game."

That visual helped me mentally prepare to play. I would repeat it to myself on the night before games, falling asleep with it going through my mind. When I ran onto the field, I was ready. Visualizing a pattern, defensive coverage, or move was a really important part of the headwork needed to prepare for the game.

By junior year I was starting every game. Bleier threw every pass I caught and I caught every pass that touched my hands. We were a force. To hear Bob describe it, "We were a nice duo. We complemented each other. We made each other famous."

I caught one pass that year that people still talk about today. It was the final game of the regular season, and a win would bring our season record to 7–3 and take us to the play-offs. We were driving down the field and were set up on the 20-yard line, hoping for a touchdown victory against the College of William and Mary. I was running a 15-yard crossing route, and Bleier threw a pass to me, but he threw it high. I jumped and one-handed the ball. I plucked it out of the air like I was Willie Mays. I was almost horizontal when the point of the ball hit me in the palm. It rolled down my arm as Mark Kelso, William and Mary's top defensive back, hammered me. Somehow, I held on to that ball in the crook of my arm. We got a first down, and eventually drove the rest of the way for the touchdown.

People still come up to me and tell me, "Leland, I'll never forget that catch."

We went to the Division 1-AA play-offs and beat Boston University in our first round of play. Unfortunately, Rhode Island knocked us out in the quarterfinals a week later. We ended the year 8–4.

All of us—the coaches, the players, and the fans— expected the next year to be even better. We trained hard in the off-season before the start of my senior year.

Seven games into my senior season, we were the number-one-ranked team in the nation in Division 1-AA and had won every game. I caught sixty-five passes, eight for touchdowns, and totaled 956 yards. It was an exciting time—we were winners, and the school loved us.

Games eight and nine, however, were hard losses against Rutgers and Boston University. It looked like our next game, against Brown, might end the same way. We had three fumbles to start the game, and by the half, the score was 13–0. I could tell my teammates thought we were facing defeat, but I wasn't ready to give up. I was team captain and I did my best to encourage everyone at halftime, letting them know that we could turn this around. It was my turn to let someone know that I believed in them.

In the second half, we stormed the field a different team—a winning team. The Spiders scored 29 unanswered points to win the game 29–13. I caught five passes for 55 yards. During this time I got an unexpected call telling me I had been selected to apply for a Rhodes Scholarship. I would be the only student that the University of Richmond would submit to the competition that year.

Seriously? I thought. *This can't be happening.*

Rhodes Scholars—there are thirty-two of them from the US in any given year—get a free ride to Oxford University in England to attend graduate school in the area of their choosing. Three years before, I was nearly expelled for violating the school's honor code, and now I was nominated for what was perhaps the most prestigious award a university could give. I would be judged not only on academics and sports, but also on my character.

The timing couldn't have been worse. The Rhodes Scholar selection process was almost as difficult as winning a spot in the astronaut corps. The first steps took place over Thanksgiving weekend, right as the Spiders were contending for a spot in the play-offs. NFL recruiters were calling to say they would be showing up in the next few weeks to check out my performance on the field. And first-semester finals were only a few weeks away.

I was one of 1,143 applicants from around the country that year. It would have been an amazing honor to have been chosen, but I was eliminated fairly early on in the process.

Back on the field, it looked like we could make it all the way to the play-offs. Our last game of the regular season was against William and Mary, just like it had been the year before. We put in a good effort, but there was no magic catch this time. We lost the game 17–23, dashing our hopes for a play-off run.

The team ended the year 8–3. I went on to become an NCAA 1-AA Academic All-American and Richmond's career leader in receptions and receiving yards. I had caught a pass in each of the thirty-nine games in which I played.

I was proud of my record—198 receptions for 2,669 yards and 16 touchdown receptions.

I was thinking about what I wanted to do after graduation as the football season was winding down.

Back on campus the following January, I remember walking to the student commons on my way from the chem lab. People were gathered around a television to watch the space shuttle *Challenger* launch. NASA was sending a teacher from Concord, New Hampshire, Christa McAuliffe, into space, so the launch had gotten a lot of attention in the media.

We were half paying attention when, only seventy-three seconds after liftoff, *Challenger* broke apart over the sunny Florida coast. Everyone was just . . . stunned. As I watched the tragedy unfold, I remember thinking to myself that someday, as a scientist, I wanted to play a part in preventing disasters like that from happening. But at that moment, the future right in front of me seemed far more earthbound.

I GET A CALL

I had decided early in my college career that medicine was not for me. My parents understood. All they really wanted for me was to be happy. At that point, I was planning to go to graduate school for chemistry.

But then I got a call that changed everything.

It was April 30, a Wednesday, and I had just taken my last final exam. Earlier that day, Joe Bushofsky, a scout for the Detroit Lions, had phoned to ask me whether I'd be home that night, and I'd told him I would be. The scout for the Denver Broncos had the same question. Exams were wrapping up and people were looking for a party, but I wasn't about to go out on a night the NFL might call.

The NFL Scouting Combine is a yearly scouting event held every February where players get a chance to show their skills to pro teams and try to get noticed for draft day—the day NFL general managers offer college players a spot on their teams.

I hadn't been invited to attend the combine, but I had gotten some attention. Pro football scouts notice when a major division college team goes from 0–10 to 8–3 in just four years. Scouts from the Detroit Lions, the Denver Broncos, and the Dallas Cowboys had all flown to Richmond to watch my games and judge my potential. They were interested, but there were no guarantees.

Then the phone rang.

"Leland Melvin?" It was Joe Bushofsky. "You have been drafted in the eleventh round of the NFL college draft. Do you want to play for the Detroit Lions?"

I had never imagined myself in the NFL, but now I had made it!

I had made it to the NFL!

"Yes, sir," I said. And I hung up the phone.

I'm generally pretty even-keeled. I don't have super highs or super lows. Instead of jumping up and down and shouting out the window, I immediately started to get ready for the NFL. I knew that just being drafted wasn't going to be enough for me. I wanted to be the best I could be. I wanted my shot to stand out.

The next day, the University of Richmond was alive with the news. Local TV news carried the story, as did the *Richmond Times-Dispatch*. School administrators and professors whom I'd never met beamed with pride during news interviews. My teammates were ecstatic; that was probably the best part of the whole thing.

My parents were also elated, although I'm pretty sure

that as much as I was preparing to make the team, my mother was warming up her prayer book. She had prayed for me throughout my college years, and now those prayers were said in hopes of keeping me from getting badly injured in the NFL.

Four days after the call, I was on a plane to Michigan for the Lions' minicamp. Minicamp is a week of intensive training that gives the coaches a chance to assess the new players and decide who's in and who's out. It's nerve-racking, especially for a guy who wasn't chosen until the eleventh round, but I didn't let that faze me. I figured I had nothing to lose. On the last day of practice, on the last play of the day, I caught a pass in the end zone right in front of head coach Darryl Rogers. I finished on a high note, confident that I would find a place on the team. I caught a plane back to Richmond, ready to graduate from college.

Graduation was a blur. I remember feeling the peacefulness that comes from having succeeded at something really hard combined with the pride about my future in the National Football League. During my four years at the University of Richmond, I had had low points and high points, but never once had I thought of giving up. Instead, through the grace and wisdom of the people in my life during those years, I developed a growth mind-set. I believed anything was possible.

Sitting in the Robins Center in my cap and gown, I

never imagined that I would be there again twenty-two years later. That I would have the chance to stand on that stage, not as a recent graduate, but as a commencement speaker. Delivering the University of Richmond's 178th commencement address—three months after I'd returned from my first mission to space—was one of the proudest moments of my life.

CHAPTER 6
MY SHORT LIFE IN THE NFL

I'd always been good at football, even at a young age. I was on the small side, but I was fast and could catch pretty much anything. When I was a kid in the 1970s, most boys played football or basketball or baseball—or all three.

My father had played football in college and later in the air force, so we both thought I would play football, too. Honestly, I enjoyed Saturday afternoons on the tennis court over Friday nights in the football stadium. But in Lynchburg in 1982, football meant college scholarships. So football it was.

Unlike many of the college recruits who arrived at minicamp, playing in the NFL wasn't my dream. I knew too well that the odds of getting into the NFL were long. Less than 1 percent of high school football players make it all the way to the pros.

But I wasn't thinking about any of that when I arrived in Rochester, Michigan, in July 1986, for the Detroit Lions' two-week training camp. Now that I'd been drafted, I wanted to be a success. First and foremost, that meant impressing the coaches. You can't rack up the stats if the coaches don't put you in the game. And the level of play in the NFL was orders of magnitude different from what I experienced in college. The guys are bigger, faster, stronger, smarter, and they're all fighting for the same few spots on the team. During that first week, a lot of players got injured. League rules say you can't get cut from the team if you are injured, and some players exaggerated injuries just to stay with the team, even if only for one more day.

This was a totally different world from Richmond. There were no hazing rituals to help us bond and become members of the team. We were all competing against one another. Veteran players feared being replaced by rookies, and rookies feared being overlooked.

Getting hurt was part of the game. In the NFL, you were expected to be a gladiator. You didn't have much of a choice; hurt or not, you got back up and went out on the field when they called your number or you went home.

In the NFL, coaches look for "the right stuff" in a player just like NASA does in an astronaut. They want to know that a player is strong enough to endure pain and injury to get the job done. The right stuff means never showing weakness, and making the tough stuff look easy, even if it takes years to develop the necessary skills and stamina.

Some scientific research suggests that elite athletes feel pain to a lesser degree than nonathletes. Elite athletes are able to push their bodies to extremes day after day. I saw that firsthand in the NFL. Players would come to the field day in and day out ready and, yes, willing to tolerate pain. In my case, I had always been able to endure a pretty high degree of discomfort. For me it was a matter of mind over matter. On the field or in the classroom, I would work as hard as needed to reach a goal—regardless of how much hurt I went through to get there. Whether I was born that way or it was an ability I developed, I can't say.

But success in the NFL, as in life, takes more than a high pain threshold. Success also depends on the kind of people you have around you. In my case, throughout my life, I had the help and support of my parents, my Lynchburg community, college teammates, professors, and coaches. They saw potential in me even when I did not. Their confidence in me gave me the confidence I needed to compete at the NFL level.

During the second week of training camp, I was running a route down the sideline, accelerating to catch a pass, when I felt a pull in my left hamstring. I winced and stumbled to the grass. In what would prove to be a stroke of luck, the trainer saw it and he pulled me out of the game.

That same trainer vouched for me later when Coach Darryl Rogers and his staff drilled him about which players were injured and which were faking it to stick around. Torn hamstrings can take as long as a year to heal. I just had a severe pull, which I hoped would only take a couple of weeks to get better. By the end of that same month—July—I was training again and playing well despite being in considerable pain at times.

Coach Rogers came to practice and said that he thought a lot of us were trying to make the team by getting on the injured reserve list. "If you don't get on the field, we're gonna cut you," he said.

I knew I wasn't fully healed, but I also knew that I had to get back out there for our preseason games if I wanted to have any shot to make the team. Chuck Long, a rookie first-round draft choice, was at quarterback. I got in the game against Philadelphia and ran a 15-yard hook. He threw the ball and I caught it. I could see excitement on the position coach's face.

I caught another pass in that preseason game against Philadelphia, and then another two against Seattle.

Unfortunately, there was another play in the Philadelphia game when we were at our 40-yard line with man-to-man coverage. I was running down the sideline trying to lose my defender, but I just didn't have the juice. I saw the pass and I dove for the ball, but it was too far in front of me.

The coach warned me not to dive after the ball like that again. "You're gonna hurt yourself," he said.

I knew that was true. My leg was worn out. Hurling myself after the ball only put a bigger strain on it.

I wasn't surprised when on the following Tuesday, someone knocked on my door. I didn't have to open the door to know what it meant. For reasons beyond explanation, in the NFL the coaches always cut players on Tuesdays, and that week was the final round of cuts before the season started.

My roommate at the time was Lyle Pickens, a rookie defensive back from the University of Colorado. Reaching the NFL had been Lyle's lifelong goal. He heard the knock and, like me, knew what was coming.

"Coach wants to see you guys. Says to bring your playbooks," the guy said.

I was on a plane home to Lynchburg that night. For me, it was a blow, but not that surprising. I was an eleventh-round draft pick with an injured hamstring—I would cut me too.

I was returning to my hometown with no immediate

plan. I had no idea what I was going to do.

It turned out that I wasn't quite done with the NFL. The following morning, I was lying in bed in my childhood room thinking about my next move when I got a call from my agent, Will Rackley.

"The Dallas Cowboys want to check you out for the next season," he said. "They want you in Dallas tomorrow."

I got cut from the Lions on Tuesday evening and the next morning I already had a call from Dallas. By that afternoon, I was on the field for my tryout, catching passes from Pro Bowl quarterback Danny White.

I flew home from Dallas on Thursday. I was hopeful, but no one had said anything to me about my performance. I had barely unpacked my bags when Rackley called again and told me that the Toronto Argonauts were interested in me. They wanted me to train with them for two weeks so they could evaluate my skills and assess my rehab.

It was a total whirlwind.

I didn't know much about Canada or about the Canadian league, but I had a friend on the team from the University of Richmond, Mark Seal. I hadn't heard back from Dallas. I figured why not check it out? So I caught a flight to Toronto Friday morning.

A few days into the Argonauts' practice, I got another call from Rackley. "Dallas wants to sign you," he told me.

I would miss the 1986 season, but the Cowboys wanted

me as a free agent for the 1987 season.

I had been given a second chance.

I was back in the NFL.

I had six months to recuperate until the Cowboys' minicamp in March. I wasn't getting paid, so I took a job in Richmond delivering packages for my agent. One afternoon I bumped into Dr. Raymond Dominey, the husband of one of my old chemistry professors at the University of Richmond. He was teaching at the University of Virginia.

"You should talk to Glenn Stoner in the UVA materials science engineering department," he said.

Materials science engineers work with metals, ceramics, plastics, and other materials to create everything from better golf clubs and tennis shoes to aircraft wings and computer chips. It's a discipline that combines chemistry and engineering, two of my interests, but at that point, I thought I was going to play for the Cowboys, not go to graduate school.

"Just go and see what he has to say," Dr. Dominey suggested.

I liked both him and his wife, so I did what he asked.

I drove to Charlottesville the next day. Years later, Dr. Dominey told me he had a hunch materials science would appeal to me—and he was right. Later I learned that aside from being a brilliant scientist, Dr. Stoner was also a huge football fan. He couldn't resist the idea of an NFL player on his staff. He offered me a job as research assistant in his lab until the start of minicamp, which sounded a lot better to me than delivering packages—and it paid better, too. I rented a room in an apartment on Fifteenth Street in Charlottesville and stayed in shape by working out with the UVA football team every day.

I felt right at home at UVA. The materials science engineering department might sound like a nerd convention, but the students there were determined to have fun. And they all seemed to love their work.

Even though I was leaving for the Cowboys' minicamp in Texas in a few months, Dr. Stoner encouraged me to apply to the graduate program. I was reluctant at first, knowing it would require long hours of studying, but I also knew that an NFL career could end even before it began. Getting started on a graduate degree would allow me to hedge my bets.

So I applied and started classes in mid-January, before my March start date with the Cowboys. Luckily for me, the engineering program at UVA had some classes that were broadcast as TV courses for remote students, and the department was kind enough to record them for me once I left for Texas. Dr. Stoner and my colleagues in the department even volunteered their help over the phone if needed.

Balancing the NFL and grad school would prove to be

the hardest thing I've ever done. The Cowboys expected me to spend ten or more hours a day conditioning in the gym and running drills on the field. And just like the Lions' camp, the players were ultracompetitive.

Most of the guys did nothing besides work out, eat, and sleep. I added on hours of schoolwork every night. Most nights I caught only a few hours of rest.

On top of graduate school lessons, I had to learn the Cowboys' playbook. Their playbook was three inches thick, and every page contained diagrams and detailed descriptions of plays. I needed to come up with a system to memorize it all quickly or there was no way I'd be able to keep up. I was running out of hours in the day.

I had learned some computer programming during high school, so I programmed electronic flashcards of the major plays into my laptop. It was a crude system—nothing I would be able to sell to Microsoft—but it got the job done.

I was stretching on the Cowboys' practice field about a month into training camp when Danny White called over to me. "Hey, rookie, let's throw," he said. Danny knew that a hamstring injury had sidelined me in Detroit, and we agreed I would run at half speed until I was warmed up to avoid reinjuring myself.

Then Tom Landry, the Cowboys' head coach, walked onto the field. Anytime a quarterback has an opportunity to impress the head coach, he's going to take it. Danny quickly changed the play and called one that required more distance. There was no way I'd catch the pass at half speed, and with Landry watching, there was no way I was going to give less than my best. *He's going to see me as an unmotivated rookie*, I thought. So I kicked it into gear and gave it everything I had. I never made it to the end zone to catch the ball. I felt a stinging pain in my upper left hamstring. I had pulled it again. I came to a stop very quickly, clutching my injured leg.

Typically, the treatment for hamstring injuries involves rest, ice, compression, and elevation. But the Cowboys' trainers were always looking for new ways to get guys back on the field, so they sent me to an acupuncturist in Dallas. I also worked intensely with a physical therapist and a trainer. I was determined to heal quickly.

The program worked brilliantly. I recovered more quickly than I'd ever expected and was ready for the team's practice schedule and for the start of preseason.

We had a few days off before heading from Texas to the Cowboys' summer training camp in Thousand Oaks, California, so I went home for a short visit. I had bulked up so dramatically in training camp that when I pulled up in front of the house and got out of my car, my parents hardly recognized me. I had been in top physical condition at the University of Richmond, but with the pros I had reached a new level, that of a perfectly tuned machine.

And I was looking forward to proving that to the team.

But shortly after I arrived in California, Coach Landry summoned me to a conference room. "And bring your playbook," I was told.

I took that as a good sign. The only time you're asked to bring your playbook is when you're getting cut or switching positions. I didn't think Landry would cut me before evaluating my performance. He hadn't seen me on the field much since I had recovered, and I was in top shape. My leg felt great. I was guessing that he had decided to move me from wide receiver to defensive back, which did not seem unreasonable.

I walked into a classroom carrying my playbook and saw Coach Landry sitting at a long table.

"Leland, I'm releasing you from the team," he said.

And with those few words, my NFL career was over before the season even started.

I can't say I wasn't angry. I felt I hadn't been given a real chance to show the team what I could do. That afternoon, I packed my things and moved to my uncle's apartment in Los Angeles, where I spent a few days sitting on the beach, contemplating what had just happened. My first thought was to keep fighting, to find myself a spot somewhere in the NFL. I had come so far. But my instincts told me otherwise. And so, just as I had done at every other turning point in my life, I asked God for direction.

With a lot of prayer and reflection, it became clear to me that it was time to turn the page and to start a new chapter in my life. I flew home to Lynchburg and found an apartment in Charlottesville in time for the fall semester at UVA. And like that, I was back to being a full-time student.

Only a week before, I had been training with the Cowboys, a fact my classmates found endlessly amusing. I was surrounded by guys wondering what it was like to play for "America's Team." And then there was Marlene Jaworski.

"You played pro football?" she asked. Marlene had a thick Boston accent, and I was pretty certain she knew nothing about football. "What team?"

"Dallas Cowboys."

"What position?"

"Wide receiver," I replied.

"I guess that means you're really . . . fast?" she asked, raising her eyebrows. I could tell she didn't have a clue what a wide receiver did.

"Uh, yeah . . . I'm pretty fast, I guess," I said.

Marlene wasn't terribly impressed—and that was a weird relief. It was nice to be in a totally different world from the one I had been living and breathing for more than a year. And like that, I closed the chapter on my life as a serious football player.

At UVA, Marlene and I formed a study group with

Brenda Jones, the student who had been sending me her class notes when I was at training camp. We called ourselves the Three Musketeers, and without the two of them, I don't think I would have survived graduate school, or had as much fun in Charlottesville.

I found a family in the materials science engineering department. Years later, I made sure to invite Dr. Dominey and Dr. George Cahen, another of my UVA professors, to watch my first shuttle launch at Cape Canaveral. Marlene and Brenda also came, though I didn't get to see any of them because astronauts are in quarantine for a week before the launch. By the time they arrived in Florida, I was isolated from anyone who might pass on germs that could make me sick in space.

Most of my colleagues from the materials science program went on to careers in manufacturing or product design, but Marlene followed a different track. She ended up teaching science in the Boston public school system. Many of her middle school students came from public housing in dilapidated neighborhoods and faced steep odds in their paths to success.

Years later, I spoke to them about the importance of staying in school. I wanted them to know that failures in life are the building blocks for later success, and that anything was possible.

Even my serendipitous path to space.

CHAPTER 7

FROM GRAD SCHOOL TO NASA

Working in Dr. Myers's lab at Richmond had turned me into a scientist. Graduate school turned me into an engineer.

Some people wonder if there's ever any conflict between my "scientist brain" and my religious faith. The simple answer to that question is no. I believe that a person can have both a strong religious faith and a strong dedication to science. At the heart of both is an attempt to explain what seems unexplainable. Science leads with the head and religion with the heart. But in my opinion, there are so many mysteries that science still can't explain—and will likely never be able to explain—and that's where my faith comes in.

In the spring of 1989, I was getting ready to graduate from UVA with a master's degree in materials science engineering.

I expected to get a job at one of the top chemical companies like DuPont or Dow Chemical. I met recruiters from both places at a career fair held by UVA. Both wanted to bring me to their offices for job interviews. I thought it would just be a matter of which company made me the best offer to do the most interesting work.

I was on my way out of the career fair when I passed a booth with the NASA logo. The next thing I knew, a black woman with a big smile and a badge that read "Rosa Webster, NASA Langley Research Center" grabbed my arm.

"What's your name?" she asked.

Who is this woman and why is she in my face? I wondered. But my mother raised me to be polite. "Leland Melvin," I said, wondering how long it would take to get away from her so I could meet Marlene and Brenda for dinner.

"Leland," she said, "you're going to work at NASA."

My first thought was, *No. I'm not going to work at NASA.* But she never gave me a chance to say so.

"I've been looking for you all day," Rosa said. "Can you help me get these things to my car?"

Once again, my mother had raised me to be polite. So even though I had no intention of working at NASA and was anxious to get to dinner, I helped Rosa close down her booth while she told me about her work.

WHO WORKS AT NASA?

Working at NASA had never crossed my mind. I mean, *who works at NASA?* Certainly nobody who looked like me. I had a stereotypical view of people who worked for the space agency—white guys with crew cuts and clipboards. I also knew the pay would be better in private industry, and I thought the opportunities would be better, too. Hearing Rosa's excitement about the cutting-edge science that was being done at NASA was interesting, but I wasn't sold that NASA was the right place for someone like me.

And Rosa could tell. She changed her pitch midstream and started talking about the strides NASA had made in hiring black scientists and engineers. The director of the Langley Research Center in Virginia, Paul Holloway, was under orders to improve diversity even more, and he took that directive seriously. Someone from his office had reached out to UVA's graduate school of engineering for recommendations, and my name wound up high on that list.

"We were looking for really strong candidates," Rosa later recalled. "I had spent the whole day thinking, 'is Leland Melvin going to show up?'"

A half hour into our talk, Rosa said NASA wanted me and that she would send me a written job offer within a few days.

A job offer? I was amazed by how fast that had happened. But competition for qualified science and technology graduates was fierce, especially minority recruits. Rosa had been given the authority to make verbal offers on the spot.

I promised Rosa I would think about it, but I still believed my future was in private industry. Over the next few days, I flew to both DuPont and Dow headquarters for interviews.

Soon after those interviews, a letter from NASA arrived with the formal job offer. And I began to think about whether I really wanted to create stronger and better tennis shoes and golf clubs, or whether I wanted to further human exploration of space.

No surprise: Space won.

Going to work for NASA didn't make me an astronaut. There are lots of different career opportunities at the space agency. They have openings for everyone, from the scientists who program our computers to the lawyers who draft our documents to the doctors who clear astronauts for space missions to the nutritionists who plan and cook meals that will be eaten in space.

NASA also operates facilities around the country with

different mission specialties and expertise. The agency's headquarters are in Washington, DC. In 1989, I went to work at NASA Langley, which is in Hampton, Virginia. Langley is dedicated to research. Astronaut training happens at the Johnson Space Center (JSC) in Houston, Texas. The Kennedy Space Center in Cape Canaveral, Florida, is where most missions are launched into space.

My first job was as a research scientist. I was tasked with developing ways to use lasers and optical fibers to detect damage on things like rocket ships and the International Space Station. The goal was to find ways to spot problems that the human eye can't see. My first job, and I was already helping the agency save time, money, and lives.

Years later, in 2003, the space shuttle *Columbia* disintegrated as it reentered Earth's atmosphere. All seven astronauts on board were killed. I wasn't directly involved in that mission, but I lost seven good friends. A brick-sized piece of foam came off the fuel tank of *Columbia* on takeoff and hit the tiles on the left wing. No one spotted the missing piece of foam. Part of the problem was that once the vehicle was in orbit, there was no way for the crew to inspect the exterior of the spacecraft for damage except with cameras and binoculars. It was easy, way too easy, to miss one random loose piece of foam that hit the wing, creating a hole that caused the shuttle *Columbia* to explode.

After that tragedy, my former branch helped develop a new way of scanning the tiles and wings while shuttles were in orbit, helping to make sure that such a disaster would never happen again.

But that comes later.

When I first went to work at NASA in 1989, one of my colleagues was a professor from the University of Maryland named Jim Sirkis.

Jim encouraged me to come to the University of Maryland to pursue a PhD in mechanical engineering. NASA was willing to fund my PhD and pay me a salary at the same time—as long as I came back to work for NASA after I became "Dr. Melvin." I guess I took a lot of convincing, but after three years at NASA I decided to go for it. But my initial hesitation should have told me something. After a year in the program, I realized my heart just wasn't in it. Friends told me to stick it out. After all, I was being paid a full salary and my tuition was being paid. But I had to trust my instincts. Being in the PhD program just didn't feel right. And so I left school and went back to NASA Langley full-time.

When I returned, I became program manager of the NASA X-33 Reusable Launch Vehicle program. We were tasked with developing a vehicle to replace the space shuttle one day. That job put me in touch with people working directly on the space program and got me started on my own path to the stars.

My team's job was to develop glass fibers that would function like nerves do in the human body. In the same way that your nerves tell you that you have a cut or that you've put your hand on something hot, the fibers would detect leaks and other damage in the space shuttle and communicate that information back to a computer brain and then to scientists on the ground in mission control. Each fiber is about 125 microns in diameter, roughly the size of a human hair. The fibers could do the inspection work of an army of humans—even better, in some ways. The fibers could detect things the human eye could never see. Our work would help astronauts get to space and back safer, faster, and more efficiently.

RACE, LANGLEY, AND KATHERINE JOHNSON

I wasn't aware of it until I joined NASA, but the space agency played a major role in the federal government's efforts to integrate the South—even when it didn't necessarily want to. One of the first efforts came straight from President Kennedy. He insisted that NASA make a black test pilot named Ed Dwight an astronaut candidate in the agency's early days. Ed never felt welcome in the program and left after President Kennedy's death. He never became an astronaut. But at least it was a start.

In the '60s, the space race was accelerating along with the Cold War with the Soviet Union and as the struggle for civil rights was erupting in the South. President Kennedy and President Johnson were both firm believers in equal rights for African-Americans. They saw the space program as a high-profile opportunity to show the world the progress that equality can unleash. That effort was instrumental in getting Katherine Johnson hired as a "human computer."

Until I went to work for NASA, I had never heard of Katherine Johnson, but she is one of the great, unsung heroes in our nation's civil rights battles. Shortly after I joined the workforce at Langley, I joined the National Technical Association (NTA). Started in 1925, the NTA was the oldest group of black scientists and engineers in the country. It was at an NTA gathering, in fact, that I met Katherine Johnson—then long retired from NASA and an absolute legend among her colleagues—for the first time.

As a child in the early part of the twentieth century, Katherine counted everything—from the steps leading up to the church to the dishes she washed to the stars she saw in the sky. Her parents knew she was different. But for African-Americans in Katherine's hometown of White Sulphur Springs, West Virginia, school only went through eighth grade. Determined that Katherine receive an education, her parents agreed that she and her mother would move 120 miles away to the nearest town that would let Katherine go to high school—a place called Institute, West Virginia.

Katherine sailed through high school in Institute, graduating at the age of fourteen, and then went on to get a degree in math from West Virginia State University at eighteen.

Katherine became a teacher after graduating. Then she heard that a nearby aeronautics laboratory was looking to hire black women mathematicians to do calculations. In 1953, she became "a computer with a skirt," one in a legion of women hired to perform complex calculations—a human computer.

Katherine's genius for math defied the norm even at NASA. She calculated the launch window for Alan Shepard's *Mercury* mission, America's first manned trip to space, and assisted in calculating John Glenn's orbit around Earth. Later in her NASA career, she worked on the space shuttle program and the Earth Resources Satellite. After retiring, she encouraged students to pursue careers in science and technology fields. Katherine's contributions to NASA went far beyond science. Perhaps her greatest gift involved her willingness to ignore anyone who attempted to stand in her way. Part of the beauty of math is that you are right or wrong. A correct answer is a correct answer. It doesn't matter if the person solving the problem is man or woman, black, white, brown, or whatever. Katherine never let anyone stand in her way—and no one could, because she was always right.

Charles Bolden, the first astronaut to head NASA and the agency's first African-American leader, took note of her determination and commended her for it. She once said, "I'm as good as anybody, but no better," Bolden recalled. "The truth, in fact, is that Katherine is indeed better. She's one of the greatest minds ever to grace our agency or our country, and because of the trail she blazed, young Americans like my granddaughters can pursue their own dreams without a feeling of inferiority."

When I met Katherine, she was retired from NASA, but her personality and powerful intelligence and amazing accomplishments continued to leave a mark on the agency. Her leadership in the NTA gave her an opportunity to mentor younger scientists like me. NASA Langley is like a little town, and after work my colleagues and I would hang out in the evenings, playing basketball or softball or meeting to discuss our work. Even though she was retired, Katherine would often show up and plant herself at the center of whatever was going on.

In 2015, President Barack Obama awarded Katherine the Presidential Medal of Freedom in a ceremony at the

White House. "In her thirty-three years at NASA," he said, "Katherine was a pioneer who broke the barriers of race and gender, showing generations of young people that everyone can excel in math and science, and reach for the stars." When I accompanied Katherine to the White House to receive her award, I thought back on how much my success depended on the vision and perseverance of Katherine and others like her. People like Dr. Walter Johnson, who helped Althea Gibson and Arthur Ashe break the color barrier in tennis, and Chauncey Spencer, without whom I might never have found my way to the space program.

In her early days at NASA, I do not believe Katherine saw herself as part of a movement. She simply wanted to do her job. But her quiet insistence on being heard in a white, male organization opened doors for every man and woman of color who came after her, including me.

Katherine's contributions were so great that a movie about her and her colleagues, *Hidden Figures*, was released in January 2017.

RELUCTANT ASTRONAUT

Even though I worked for NASA, being stationed at Langley was a world away from being an actual astronaut. In 1995, Tom Kashangaki, a NASA engineer and good friend of mine, told me I should apply to the astronaut corps. He thought I had the right stuff, but I said no. The odds seemed too long and the process too time-consuming. I was happy doing what I was doing. Going to space seemed like a crazy dream.

Then my friend and colleague Charles Camarda applied and, to my surprise, was accepted. Charlie didn't exactly fit the picture I had of a NASA astronaut. He's only about five feet four inches tall, and where most astronauts will tell you they always dreamed of being an astronaut, Charlie would tell you he wanted to be either a boxer or a research scientist. But like it was for so many of us at Langley, the lure of space proved too much to resist. Charlie took the plunge, applied for the astronaut class of 1996, and was accepted. Eventually, Charlie would fly on space shuttle *Discovery*'s first mission after the *Columbia* disaster—known as the Return to Flight Mission—a flight that took extraordinary courage. Charlie would prove himself time and again to be an excellent mission specialist and engineer. But at that moment in 1996, his acceptance made me rethink my goals.

If Charlie can do it, I thought, *so can I.*

About a year into his training, Charlie flew from Houston to Langley in a sleek blue-and-white NASA T-38 training aircraft piloted by astronaut John Young. Young had flown almost every aircraft known to man and flew on every space vehicle from *Mercury* to *Apollo*, and at the time, he was probably the most decorated astronaut still active in the space program. He walked on the moon in 1972 and commanded the first space shuttle mission STS-1, *Columbia*, in 1981.

On the day they visited Langley, I had a chance to show Charlie and John the research I was doing to improve safety in the space program. I didn't know it at the time, but Charlie had told John that he should consider me as an astronaut candidate. He knew that John's input during the selection process could prove invaluable. But wouldn't you know it, John slept through my entire talk. He was John Young, so nobody dared wake him. He seemed to have a sixth sense that told him when the meeting was over. He woke up and turned to me as if he hadn't been sleeping. "Great job, Leland," he said. "You should apply to be an astronaut."

Becoming an astronaut is not easy. The numbers vary for every astronaut class depending on how many new astronauts the agency feels it needs for its upcoming missions. In my year, there were about 2,500 applicants for only 25 positions. The requirements for becoming an astronaut have gone through several changes since the first class was selected in 1959. Back then, President Eisenhower required that all astronauts be military-trained pilots. That rule was in place until 1965, when the pool expanded to include candidates chosen for their science and academic backgrounds. When I was selected, NASA was looking for scientists and engineers as well as pilots and commanders.

If I'm being honest, the first requirement for an astronaut candidate is patience. It takes forever for the pool of applicants to be whittled down. The initial cut is the largest, but also probably the easiest. From there, things get slow and serious. It begins with an interview at the Johnson Space Center that lasts for five days. That process begins with a battery of psychological tests, which includes spending time in a Personal Rescue Sphere—basically a big beach ball connected to oxygen with an umbilical hose— to see if candidates suffer from claustrophobia. As you can imagine, there's nothing worse than a claustrophobic astronaut. When you're in space, you're trapped on your ship for as long as your mission lasts. There's no going outside to get some air!

If you pass that, you get to take what seems like every medical test known to man. That's followed by intense hand-eye coordination tests to see if candidates can handle the robotics part of astronaut training.

And if that isn't stressful enough, the selection committee uses every interaction (and I mean EVERY interaction) with NASA personnel to test and evaluate a candidate's character. Being rude to the janitor cleaning the bathroom could be a strike against you. Telling off the checkout person at the cafeteria could be enough to get your application denied. I recall getting fitted for a flight suit and seeing Charlie Precourt, then head of the astronaut corps, lurking in the background, eavesdropping on my conversation with the technicians.

After all that, my own interview process ended with an hour-long talk with the selection committee. My committee members included John Young, senior NASA leaders, administrators, and five highly decorated navy pilots. I don't usually get nervous, but that day, man, was I sweating.

When the questioning started, a committee member had to catch me when I leaned too far back in my chair and almost fell over.

Each candidate is required to write an essay explaining what they can contribute to the human exploration of space. I began my essay by discussing the values I learned from my parents. "At the age of five, my father drove me to my first Little League basketball practice," I wrote, "where he emphatically stressed for me to work hard, have fun, and share the ball. Those few simple words have resonated in my head countless times throughout my school years and professional life. Though simple, they emanated the commitment and selflessness required to work and play as a team. My parents taught me early on that virtues such as courage, integrity, and faith were assets that would guarantee success. By fully embracing these values, they assured me that being myself would be enough. Therefore, I offer myself to be used further in the human exploration of space, like so many others before me."

The committee also asked me to trace the path of my candidacy, starting with high school. I'm sure a lot of applicants talked about how they'd wanted to be an astronaut their whole lives, but that wasn't the case with me. When I was growing up, the space race was in full throttle, and at night my dad would take me outside to look at the sky. I was fifteen years old when Guion Bluford became the first African-American astronaut, and nineteen when he first traveled to space. But until I worked at NASA Langley, it had never crossed my mind to become an astronaut, just as I'd never imagined I'd play in the NFL until the Lions were about to draft me.

I responded to a range of questions, including queries about my experience handling certain tools, my manual dexterity, and how I'd dealt with some of the hardest times in my life. I had no idea how it was going because all of my interrogators were careful not to give any hint of what they thought.

After completing the interviews, the selection committee met with the twenty or so astronaut candidates in a less formal environment. These "socials" took place at Petey's, a NASA hangout. At Petey's I got the opportunity to meet George Abbey, a shy engineer who spoke so softly you had to get real close just to hear him, but who also happened to be the director of the Johnson Space Center. It was widely known that getting a few minutes of face time with Abbey could help your chances. And, in a stroke of luck for me, it turned out that he was a huge Dallas Cowboys fan.

I left Houston hopeful, but still thinking that spending any time off the planet was a long shot.

But then . . . It was a sunny morning in June 1998. I remember it like it was yesterday. We were making fiber sensors in the Optics Lab at NASA Langley. My team had just finished the first optical fiber sensor, and everybody was feeling great about our work. Years of effort from dozens of different scientists had gone into the project. Yes, it was a small piece of a much larger project, but I took a great deal of pride and satisfaction in knowing that my work could save lives.

I was in the lab when I got a message to call Ken "Taco" Cockrell, chief of the astronaut office. And I knew. I just knew. In astronaut culture, there are two calls that you never forget: The one informing you that you've been accepted into the astronaut corps and the one informing you that you've been assigned a spot on a mission—that you're going to space. My whole life was about to change.

I called him back, but the call got dropped. Then it happened again. This wasn't a good sign. I dialed Ken Cockrell's number a third time, and he picked up on the third ring.

"Leland, how's it going?" Cockrell asked.

Small talk, I realized. *He must be trying to let me down easy, I'm sure of it.*

"Fine, Ken. How are you?"

Ken paused for what seemed like minutes. *Was he messing with me?*

"I'm calling to tell you that we'd like you to be part of the astronaut corps. Do you want to be part of the astronaut corps?"

Anyone who knows me will tell you that I'm always even-keeled—but this moment was different. I might not have been jumping up and down and yelling like a maniac, but this was a high point of my life.

"Yes, definitely. That's great," I said. I remember thinking to myself, *Wow, I'm an astronaut candidate. Okay, I'm ready. Let's go.*

CHAPTER 8
THE WORLD'S MOST EXCLUSIVE CLUB

The hardest thing any astronaut candidate hears comes right after they invite you to join the astronaut corps. As soon as you say yes, they tell you, "Great. Now don't tell *anybody*."

The NASA communications office wants to break the news. They ask that you don't even tell your parents until after NASA has talked to the press.

So I sat alone in my office, knowing that I'd just heard the most life-changing news of my whole life—and I couldn't tell a soul. That lasted for about five minutes. This news was just too big, and I figured that my friends at

NASA could keep a secret—at least for a few hours.

"Hey, guys! I made it into the astronaut corps!" I called out to my team.

And then I called my parents.

My mother, as she always did, told me she loved me and was proud of me. I knew she was already starting to wrap her head around the risk and the danger that came along with space exploration. Lots of prayers wouldn't be far behind.

When she handed the phone to my father, I choked up a little. My father usually had lots to say. But on this day, for this news, he was quiet. He was too proud for words.

From the day in 1961 that Russian cosmonaut Yuri Gagarin became the first person to orbit Earth, through the end of 2016, only 565 people have flown to space.

Twenty-five astronauts were chosen from a pool of about 2,500 applicants to be in my class of 1998. They added six international astronauts to bring the total to thirty-one members. Most of those who made it into the program had been turned away before, some more than a dozen times. And yet somehow the former pro football player with no long-smoldering dream to travel into space got in on his very first try.

The NFL Players Association calculates that the chances of a high school player making it to the NFL are about 0.2

My family portrait, 1966.

Me as four-year-old, 1968.

Cat and I color while my mom sleeps in the living room.

Camping with family and having a great time.

My high school freshman-year class picture.

The Perrymont football team, fall 1975. I'm number 47!

The Heritage High School tennis team, spring 1981.

The game-winning
catch that earned me
a scholarship to the
University of Richmond.

Me on the cover of
the University of
Richmond magazine
with my Spider
teammates, 1985.

Courtesy of University of Richmond

Spiders

RICHMOND
VS
NORTHEASTERN

Oct. 19, 1985
$1.50

FOOTBALL MAGAZINE

Jeff McLean

John Henry

James Church

RICHMOND 23

RICHMOND

RICHMOND 92

RICHMOND 4

RICHMOND 20

Leland Melvin

Brian Shields

Catch The Action . . . Homecoming 1985
"There's No Place Like Home"

The 1998 Penguin class of astronauts at the Johnson Space Center,
Houston, TX.

Me using a computer. See how different they used to look!

Michelle Obama

Barack Obama (signature)

Meeting President Barack Obama and First Lady Michelle Obama.

Hanging out with Jake and Scout after a run in McNair Memorial Park, El Lago, TX.

A photo with my STS-122 crew at the Johnson Space Center, 2007.

STS-122 and Expedition 16 crew members pose for a group photo following a joint news conference in the Columbus Laboratory of the International Space Station while space shuttle Atlantis *is docked with the station. From the left (bottom) are NASA astronaut Stephen Frick, STS-122 commander; and Peggy Whitson, Expedition 16 commander. From the left (middle row) are NASA astronaut Dan Tani, STS-122 mission specialist; ESA astronaut Léopold Eyharts, Expedition 16 flight engineer; and cosmonaut Yuri Malenchenko, Expedition 16 flight engineer representing Russia's Federal Space Agency. From the left (top row) are NASA astronaut Stan Love, ESA astronaut Hans Schlegel, NASA astronauts me, Rex J. Walheim, all STS-122 mission specialists; and Alan "Dex" Poindexter, STS-122 pilot.*

percent. The chances of being an astronaut are actually far less. And on that day in 1998, I became the only person ever to have been drafted by a professional football team and to be invited by NASA to train for space travel.

People ask me all the time how I managed to succeed against such staggering odds. The better question is, why does *anybody* succeed? Is it that people are born with a certain set of abilities, the right stuff? Or is it less about talent and more about attitude?

It's a hard question to answer, but I'll be honest and say that I never felt like I was blessed with that much natural ability. I always believed that I could be anything, do anything if I wanted it badly enough. My parents and other role models in my community showed me that hard work and dedication are all you really need to succeed. Without that deeply held belief, I don't think I would have achieved even half of what I have attempted.

Nothing is impossible. If you believe in yourself and put your whole heart into whatever you do, you'll be a success.

ASTRONAUT TOWN

After I got word of my acceptance, I had two months before I needed to report to the Johnson Space Center in Houston. And I needed all that time—because moving to Houston is like moving to another world. There's the unbearable heat, bad drivers, and a level of racial prejudice that astonished me. And if you've never been to southern Texas, you don't know cockroaches. Texas cockroaches are humongous! They were one of the first things I noticed when I settled into my new home in Houston. And they flew. *Huge, flying cockroaches. Crazy.*

I bought a house in El Lago, the neighborhood where Neil Armstrong and Buzz Aldrin lived at the time of the first moon landing. El Lago City Hall has an Astronaut Wall of Fame with photos of all the astronauts who had lived there—forty-eight at last count, including me. The house I found was simple but beautiful. And I remember thinking, *I could get used to this.*

On the other hand, some people had to get used to me. El Lago wasn't a place that had seen a lot of black people, let alone many black astronauts. The day I moved in, a woman across the street stared at me, her arms folded across her chest.

"Hi!" I said, and waved to her.

She shook her head and walked back into her house.

Thanks for the warm welcome, neighbor.

BECOMING A PENGUIN

Men wanted for hazardous journey. Small wages, bitter cold, long months of complete darkness, constant danger. Honor and recognition if successful.

Legend has it that Sir Ernest Shackleton, the great explorer, ran this ad in the *Times of London* newspaper when he set out to find the perfect crew for his 1913 expedition to the South Pole. He got 5,000 responses for 28 positions. I'm quite certain that if the men and women in the 1998 astronaut candidate class had seen it, they all would have answered that ad.

It's a tradition in the astronaut program for the previous class to give a nickname to the new class. Our predecessors were called the Sardines because at forty-five candidates, they were the largest single astronaut class ever. They always had to squeeze in tight for group pictures. The Sardines chose to call us the Dodos, after the flightless bird. They said it would be a while before any of us ever flew. We weren't thrilled to be associated with an animal that is not only extinct, but also really ugly. We changed our name to the Penguins. We were still named for a flightless bird, but at least a much more lovable one.

On my first night in Houston, my astronaut class met for a reception at the home of one of our class members, Gregory "Ray J." Johnson, a retired navy captain. An aerospace engineer and research pilot, Ray J. had worked at the Johnson Space Center since 1990. He became our class leader, along with army helicopter pilot Timothy "TJ" Creamer. TJ was an army aviator who had worked in the space shuttle program for three years before becoming an astronaut candidate.

All together, we Penguins were made of military-trained pilots, research scientists, one schoolteacher (Barbara Morgan), and six candidates who came from around the world. Looking around the room, you couldn't have guessed what we had in common. Still, from that moment forward, everything we did was designed to turn us into an unbreakable team.

But that would take time. That first year of training is tough. You're just a rookie. In NASA terms, you're an astronaut candidate—or an "AsCan." For many of us, it was the first time we weren't the smartest person in the room. In many ways, it reminded me of my experience in the NFL, catching passes from people like Danny White. The difference, I hoped, was that this time I'd go all the way . . . to space.

It didn't take long before I was steeped in the astronaut world. NASA's culture of perfection is humbling at first, but it reinforces the awesome responsibility that comes with becoming a space traveler. NASA invests tens of millions of dollars to train a single astronaut. It wasn't until that first day at JSC that it hit me that I was joining an elite club. Leland Melvin, the unexpected astronaut.

The first year of AsCan training involves moving from

one activity to another, like kids at summer camp. Boats! Planes! Swimming lessons! Seriously. Passing a swimming test is something we have to do in our first month. Unless you can swim three lengths of a 25-meter pool without stopping, you might as well go home. If you pass that test, then you have to do it all over again in a flight suit and tennis shoes. I also had to tread water for ten minutes wearing my flight suit. I think I drank about half the pool, but I passed.

From there we moved on to water survival training, something we had to learn before we could do any kind of flying. Scuba training was required as well, to prepare us for spacewalk training.

One of the most interesting things we did was to fly in what is affectionately known as the "Vomit Comet." This modified jet performs parabolic maneuvers, which basically means it flies very fast in U-shaped curves. That maneuver leaves you feeling weightless, just like you would be in space, for about twenty seconds. The aircraft repeats this maneuver as many as forty times in a row. That tends to lead to some upset stomachs—ergo, the plane's nickname. I'm happy to say that in all my flights on the Vomit Comet, I didn't lose my cookies once.

The plane can also mimic the gravity on the moon (which has about 16 percent of Earth's gravitational pull) and on Mars (38 percent of Earth's gravitational pull). Once, while we were "on Mars," I did push-ups with six of my classmates on my back.

Then there's robotics, spacewalk training, and time in the space shuttle simulator. The list goes on and on. The training is endless and exhausting, but ultimately absolutely essential.

But it was flying in the jet that got me the most stoked. The T-38 is NASA's two-seat, twin-engine supersonic flying machine. It's been a fixture at the Johnson Space Center since the 1980s. It trains you to think fast and adapt to changing situations—while wrenching through three Gs—or three times the force of gravity—at 40,000 feet in the air.

Even a non-pilot mission specialist like me has to learn how to fly the jet and develop navigation skills. It was essential that we all "got our mins," our quarterly minimum flight time in the jet to demonstrate our skills. AsCans have to spend at least forty-five hours in the T-38s per quarter. That's a lot of flying!

I had some of my best moments in the backseat of a NASA T-38. I remember so clearly this one time, on a beautiful Monday morning in May, I was sitting low in the backseat when I caught a glimpse of Mike Anderson in his rearview mirror smiling like he was just completely happy. Mike was one of only two other African-American astronauts at NASA when I was an AsCan, but he was the only African-American "front-seater" during that time. "Front-seaters" were military-trained pilots.

In 1998, Mike took his first shuttle flight aboard *Endeavor*, delivering equipment and fresh water to the Mir space station. A few years later, in 2003, he was fatefully assigned to be the payload commander aboard *Columbia*, a flight from which he would never return.

But when we took to the air that special May morning, the sky was full of the kind of bright, billowy clouds that blow in after a big thunderstorm. We'd been cleared to ascend to 40,000 feet, but Mike had no intention of taking the direct route. Rather, he steered the jet toward the sun and banked through the clouds like he was gliding through fresh snow. It was just . . . perfect.

Another time I was getting my minutes in with Jim Wetherbee, a navy aviator who had already flown four shuttle missions—one as pilot and three as commander—and who would later fly two more. Jim was known to be tough on AsCans.

People were afraid to fly with him because they knew that if you made a mistake, it could affect your getting assigned a space flight. And Wetherbee made a point to watch and analyze your every move. If you made a mistake in his plane, he would count it against your readiness to fly in the space shuttle without a second thought. He expected you to know how everything worked, even if you never operated the equipment. NASA makes a big deal about having all its astronaut candidates develop what they call "situational awareness." They want to make sure you know what's going on around you at all times. They want you to be able to identify problems even before they arise.

Wetherbee liked to put us in situations to test our limits, so most AsCans did everything they could to avoid flying with him because he helped determine who would fly in space. One bad day in the jet and his perception of you may be ruined.

And yet there I was, in the backseat of Wetherbee's plane, in charge of setting the altitude alerts, which tell you when you're nearing a certain height above ground level. If you were out of your intended range, a recorded voice would issue a warning.

On that day, we were "cleared for flight level 1-8-0," or 18,000 feet. But first we had to have a visual confirmation that there were no aircraft above us. I dialed in 180 and informed Wetherbee, who replied, "I see it." I took that to mean that he saw the traffic above, when in fact he was merely confirming that he'd seen me dial in our target altitude.

Luckily, there were no aircraft in our path, and there were no serious consequences. That mistake scared me.

At the same time, I'm sure it made me a better, more careful navigator. There is no room for mistakes like that in space. It's scary but true: One small overlooked detail can lead to catastrophe.

CHAPTER 9
EARNING MY WINGS

With all the flying we did in the T-38, NASA wanted to make sure we could survive if our plane went down in a remote area. Every astronaut class is subject to intense water-survival and land-survival training. Land-survival training has two purposes—to make sure we could survive in the wilderness if our plane went down and to test our ability to handle things in the ultimate wilderness, outer space.

Near the end of my first year as an AsCan, I flew to Brunswick, Maine, for four days of survivalist training. As the plane made its final approach to land at the small airstrip, I noticed the dense forest and rugged peaks below.

Looks cold, I remember thinking.

Along with my entire class of Penguins, Paige Maultsby, assistant manager of astronaut candidate training; Duane Ross, head of astronaut selection; and astronaut Robert "Beamer" Curbeam Jr., came along to guide us through our survival exercises. A team of psychologists came with us as well. They watched our every move to assess our attitude and skills. We had to show them that we could get along with each other on short trips in stressful situations if we were going to have any shot at longer stays on the International Space Station. We had to prove that we could be leaders when needed, and that we could also be followers in the right situation. We all had different strengths and different skills, and we all needed to be able to let others take command when necessary. That's not always easy when you are used to being in the lead. Survival training did more than prepare us for emergency situations. It helped make the Penguins a team.

I was paired with Sunita Williams, a navy test pilot and triathlete. She was the toughest and most competent partner you'd ever want. During a stint on the International Space Station in 2012, Sunita became the first person to ever complete a triathlon *in space*.

The two of us were an odd couple, the military test pilot and the research scientist, but we learned how to navigate, read maps, build a shelter, start a fire from scratch, and even hunt for our own food. A driving rain on the second day and night kept us from getting much sleep, but other than that it wasn't too bad. Except for the part with the rabbit.

Sitting around our campground in a forest clearing, we watched our trainer, a Navy SEAL, reach into a box and pull out a jackrabbit he had brought with him. He killed it with a whack on the head and told us all about the nutritional benefits of various organs like the kidneys and the heart while he skinned it. Then he asked for a volunteer to eat the rabbit's *eyeball*. He said it was a good source of salt and protein and could keep you alive if your vehicle went down. Clayton Anderson, a Penguin who was eager to impress the brass as well as his fellow AsCans, popped the slimy eyeball into his mouth.

I was glad Clay volunteered to eat that eyeball so I wouldn't have to.

At the end of my first year of training, I had been 40,000 feet up in the air doing three Gs in a jet, I'd endured scuba diving in freezing-cold waters, and my water- and land-survival training was complete. I'd also had basic space shuttle, space station, and robotics training.

NASA celebrated our achievements in our training course by awarding each AsCan their astronaut pin to wear on their uniform. "Unflown" astronauts receive a silver pin. "Flown" astronauts are pinned with a gold version by their commander after their first trip to space.

My new goal was to replace that silver pin with a gold one as soon as I could, and the next immediate step was to choose a technical focus for my second year of training.

STAR CITY

As we began our second year of training, NASA instructors described the different areas for candidate assignments and specializations. Every astronaut candidate was asked to write down our top three choices.

Choices ranged from the robotics branch to the International Space Station, space shuttle operations, safety, and the EVA (or spacewalk) branch to capsule communications.

We all knew that some of us would be needed in Russia on the ISS team. They'd already selected the three-person crew of Expedition 1 and were training them to become the first long-duration occupants of the brand new International Space Station. Liftoff was scheduled for October 31, 2000. The crew would fly on a Russian Soyuz rocket from the launchpad at the Baikonur Cosmodrome in Kazakhstan. Before the launch could take place, a million things needed to happen, most of them in Russia, and there was little doubt that NASA would want some of us in Moscow.

The Expedition 1 crew consisted of two Russian cosmonauts, Yuri Gidzenko, a lieutenant colonel in the Russian Air Force, and flight engineer Sergei Krikalev. The sole American crew member, Bill "Shep" Shepherd, would be the commander of the International Space Station.

As one of the few unmarried astronaut candidates in the Penguin class, I knew NASA would see me as a prime candidate for working with the ISS branch in Russia. I worried that spending a year abroad in the role of crew support, rather than working at the Johnson Space Center training, would delay my own journey to space. But Expedition 1 was the cornerstone mission of the ISS occupation, and I wanted to do my part to help make it a success.

Needless to say, going to Russia wasn't my top choice. My first choice was working with the extravehicular activity branch, which meant spacewalk training. I thought that might speed up my chances of a mission assignment. It was also the most sought-after assignment—and one that rookies rarely received.

I listed the International Space Station branch as my second choice. Astronauts in the ISS branch signed up for longer-duration stays in space, running the space station and supporting the mission specialists who arrived to do experiments or carry out specific tasks. The ISS branch could mean a trip to Russia, but I knew I was probably on the short list for ISS anyway.

I put the robotics branch down as my third choice. Robotics were responsible for designing and developing robotic hardware and software for specific missions, like using the robotic arm to install new modules on the outside of the space station.

Needless to say, I wasn't surprised when I got a call from Stephen Oswald in the astronaut office at Johnson telling me I'd been assigned to the ISS branch and I would be going to Moscow to be what they liked to call a "Russian Crusader."

At first I wasn't thrilled about the assignment, but by the time I landed in Moscow on a warm summer day in 1999, I'd come to realize that I was embarking on a once-in-a-lifetime adventure. In Moscow, I worked with Russian interpreters to help translate the procedures for the Soyuz and the ISS from Russian into English. These files contained the procedures that NASA astronauts would need to follow. The translations had to be perfect. One mistake could cost lives. My job was to make sure the English instructions worked by testing them in a computer simulation and then, finally, in a simulated space station.

I didn't stay in Moscow long. About a month after I arrived, I got a call from Houston asking me to go to Star City to help take care of astronaut Bill Shepherd. Shep was going to be the commander of Expedition 1, the first crew on the International Space Station.

Shep had spent almost two years living and training in Star City. The compound, nestled deep in a birch forest, is 15 miles outside of Moscow. It had once been a heavily guarded military base, and it still felt a lot like one when I arrived.

Shep was a great guy, but when he wanted something he could be a bulldozer. As the commander of the mission, he had to make sure everything—and I mean everything—was perfect. From the software to the procedures to the vehicle itself, if something went wrong in orbit, it was his responsibility. Sometimes Shep would get into arguments with the instructors, flight controllers, or other people in charge of getting this mission off the ground. My job was to be the buffer between Shep and everyone else. His need to be involved in even the smallest detail of the upcoming launch was challenging for the crew, but honestly I understood his concern. Decisions made now could literally mean life or death for him and his crew during the mission.

Inside NASA, if you knew only one thing about Bill Shepherd, it was probably this: During his interview for the astronaut corps in 1984, the former Navy SEAL was asked if he had any special skills they should know about. He reportedly said, "I know how to kill somebody with a knife twenty different ways." That answer alone made Shep something of a legend. Even today, if a Navy SEAL makes it to the interview level, someone will ask, "Can you kill someone with a knife, too?"

I moved into Star City with Shep. The accommodations at Star City were pretty basic. When NASA realized they would need to house astronauts there for long periods of time, they decided to build three comfortable town houses. That's where Shep and I lived. For the next fifteen months I flew back and forth from Moscow to Houston, supporting Shep in both locations.

My job was to accompany Shep on his training exercises in the simulators and wherever else he wanted to go. That sometimes included brisk, cold walks to a lake on the grounds of Star City. Shep would share what he knew about drawing and painting while I taught him photography principles and techniques. I had loved photography since middle school and took my camera along with me everywhere, a hobby that would serve me well when I flew to space.

Along the way I got to know Shep and discovered that the habits other people sometimes found annoying or controlling were grounded in his love for NASA and for his crew. He was in charge of a new multibillion-dollar outpost in space. His actions could determine the future of the space program and life or death for him and his crew. That was a huge responsibility, and he took it very seriously. I came to appreciate how his attention to detail and his refusal to accept anything less than perfection from the people he worked with was born from his commitment to the mission he'd agreed to embark upon.

My obsession with photography that year, coupled with my need to get away from Star City now and then, took me all over Moscow. I had been warned about the city's potential dangers. Russian police were known to confiscate passports and then leave you in a place where their buddies could come along and rob you. Taxi drivers did the same. The year before I arrived, a gang of skinheads had beaten up a black marine, knocking out two of his teeth. But I felt relatively safe, despite getting stares wherever I went. Even though Moscow was something of a tourist destination for western Europeans and Americans, I almost never saw another black person. I don't think I'd ever been quite as aware of myself as I was wandering the streets of Moscow then.

One Saturday afternoon, I set out for an outdoor market in Filevsky Park, along the Moskva River. The market was full of young people and loud heavy-metal music. Everyone seemed to have multiple tattoos and shaved heads. I passed through a security gate and headed for the back of the market, where it was quieter. That's when I noticed about a dozen of the skinheads staring at me.

There was an almost imperceptible nod, and I realized the skinheads had plans for me. I needed to get out of there, fast. I turned and ran for the exit. They raced after me.

Like running for that touchdown pass years ago, my speed kicked in. This time my hamstring didn't fail me. I shook them off when I reached the security gate at the entrance.

NASA had trained me to avoid fixating on problems and to be alert; to avoid mistakes before they became mistakes. My astronaut training saved me from what could have been a dangerous encounter and maybe even an international incident.

The day of the launch finally arrived: October 31, 2000. Shep and I flew from Star City to Kazakhstan, just across Russia's southern border. The Baikonur Cosmodrome, Russia's space launch facility, sits on a vast, dry plain, 20 miles from the nearest town in the middle of what could only be described as a wasteland. Shep was in good spirits. He had prepared for this for three years and was eager to get on with the mission: being the first crew to stay on the International Space Station. Shep would be stationed out in space for almost four and a half months.

After the successful launch, I stayed on in Star City for a few months. I wanted to make sure that everything went smoothly for the crew of the ISS. I didn't return home from Russia until just after Christmas Day 2000.

THE PROPHECY

As an astronaut in training, you always took note of airport runway lengths. One of the perks of the job is that if you could find 7,500 feet of asphalt, you could get a pilot buddy to fly you in a NASA T-38 just about anywhere you needed to go. But on the day I returned to Lynchburg, I had to take a commercial flight because the Lynchburg Airport only had 5,500 feet of tarmac.

I had four days before I was to report for extravehicular activity training at the Neutral Buoyancy Laboratory at the Johnson Space Center—just enough time to help celebrate my parents' thirty-fifth wedding anniversary. Here, I had a new assignment—to chauffeur the out-of-town guests to their hotel and help them get settled.

I drove my cousin Phyllis McLymore, her mother, and an unexpected passenger, Jeannette Williamson Suarez, to a hotel in downtown Lynchburg. As soon as we got there, a sudden downpour made it nearly impossible to get out of the car.

While we waited, they asked about my life as an astronaut. Then, out of the blue, with the fire and brimstone of a Southern Baptist preacher, Jeannette called my name and said she needed to share something with me. I had just met Jeannette. I didn't know she was a minister near the small town of Roseboro, North Carolina, where my father had grown up.

I turned toward Jeannette, who was in the backseat, and she looked me square in the eye.

"I have a prophecy for you," she told me. She said that

something unexpected was about to happen to me. Experts around the world would not understand why it happened. Yet I would overcome this setback and I would fly in space. This would be "my testimony to share with the world," she said.

This was a heavy message to hear considering the future I was working toward. In just four days I was going to start my EVA training in the six-million-gallon Neutral Buoyancy Laboratory pool to see if I had "the right stuff" to perform spacewalks.

I listened to Jeannette out of respect, even though I did not know her and I had never had someone share a prophecy with me before. She had a divine nature about her and a seriousness and truth to her delivery. I didn't believe she was a fake, but still her words didn't scare me. I didn't know exactly what to think about her message, but I thanked her when she was done. The spring showers dissipated and the sun peeked out from the clouds.

Four days later, I put on the puffy white EVA suit and was lowered into the pool at the Neutral Buoyancy Lab ready to start my journey as a future space walker, never once worried that Jeannette's prophecy was about to come true.

CHAPTER 10

RECOVERY AND TRAGEDY

The "something unexpected" that Jeannette had foreseen turned out to be a pretty accurate description of my hearing loss.

After my release from the hospital, I spent the next few weeks recovering at home in El Lago, Texas. I slowly began to regain hearing in my right ear but not much in my left. I struggled to regain my balance and calm—and to figure out my place in the world. If I couldn't be an astronaut, then what would I do? Despite Jeannette's promise that I would overcome my setback, some days I fell into despair. I felt so close, and now I didn't think I was ever going to fly on a mission to space. I didn't know if I would ever hear normally again. And bad hearing would keep me medically disqualified from flight.

During my second week at home, I got a visit from Eileen Collins, who had been the first female space shuttle commander and who was later the commander of the first shuttle flight after the *Columbia* accident.

"It's going to be okay," Eileen said to me that day. She had the confidence of an air force test pilot and the warmth of a mother. "If there's anything that you need, I'm here for you."

Eileen was one of the few visitors I was allowed during this period. The astronaut office had advised people to avoid visits, as they might slow down my recovery. The solitude was fine by me. My brain was trying to rewire itself to hear again, and I was trying to figure out what my life in the corps would look like as a partially deaf astronaut.

Did I lose my faith? "Lost" may be too strong a description, but I did question it. It was a dark time for me. I'd been chasing space for so long. I'd worked so hard. I couldn't help but wonder why this had happened to me. The accident made me doubt things I'd never doubted before. *Is there really a God? And if so, why would God let this happen to me? Why wouldn't that God want me to fly in space?*

In the midst of it all, I learned that Patty Hilliard

Robertson, a member of the Penguin class and a close friend, had been critically injured during the crash of a small plane. She was in the hospital fighting for her life, and her husband, Scott, asked me to come visit her. Patty was in an induced coma; she wasn't expected to survive.

Patty was a close friend. She'd brought me sushi in my hospital room when I'd first been injured. She loved food almost as much as I did. She was a classic NASA over-achiever. Patty was a doctor before she became an astronaut candidate. She had left a thriving pediatric practice to fulfill her lifelong dream of flying in space. Like me, she had been working hard to earn her first flight assignment.

Scott and I prayed together in the hospital's chapel. Sudden loss is like a punch to the gut, leaving you almost out of breath, disoriented, doubled over. I knew Scott was hoping I could help him understand why this terrible thing had happened.

After we prayed, I offered him the best words I could find. I don't honestly remember what they were, only that I hoped they gave him some comfort. I clearly remember leaving him at Patty's side after our prayer. She was surrounded by her family.

She died later that afternoon, much too soon. Patty was just thirty-eight.

After Patty's funeral, I started to rethink my own fascination with pushing the limits, with traveling to space.

There is a famous Greek myth about a boy named Icarus. Icarus and his father, Daedalus, tried to fly using wings Daedalus had built from feathers and wax. Daedalus warned Icarus not to fly too low or too high. The sea's dampness would clog his wings and the sun's heat would melt them. Icarus ignored his father's warnings and flew too close to the sun. When the wax in his wings melted, he plunged into the sea. I wondered if I had exhibited the same fatal flaws as Icarus. Had I been guilty of too much ambition? Was wanting to go to space a mistake? Was I tempting fate?

I did more soul-searching as spring rolled into summer. It was normal for astronauts to change branches and to rotate to different jobs every couple of years to learn a new set of skills. In July 2001, I was assigned to the robotics branch. Given my hearing loss, robotics was the best branch for me. Even if I couldn't fly, becoming a robotics expert would make me valuable to the corps.

I had recovered enough hearing to appear normal, but I still felt like there were wires being connected in my brain. I had to learn to position my head just right whenever I was around a lot of people so I could hear conversations.

My fellow Penguins were starting to get assigned to space missions. I wanted to celebrate with them. But at the same time, I'll be honest, I wondered if it would ever happen for me.

* * *

After my hearing stabilized, I started training in the single system trainers, or SSTs. The space shuttle and the space station are big, complex vehicles with lots of interconnected parts. Single system trainers—replicas of various systems on the shuttle and the station—allow astronauts to train on one piece of the puzzle at a time before they have to put everything together. I learned about things like the shuttle's electrical systems, computer systems, and auxiliary power units one part at a time.

Should anything ever go wrong in space, it's vital that every astronaut on board know how *all* the individual systems work. There's no time to scan the electrical switches, for instance, to find the right one. You have to *know*. Training alone in the SSTs allows us to know each system in depth before we have to start putting everything together.

After spending all that time in Russia and recovering from my accident, it sometimes felt like I was starting over from the beginning. Instructors threw all kinds of malfunctions at me, and I "fried" myself a number of times, but gradually it started to come together.

And then September 11 happened. I remember exactly where I was when I first heard the news. I had been working through a series of computer malfunctions in the SST when astronaut chief Kent Rominger summoned me to his office to tell me that something had happened in New York. The TV was on and I could see smoke pouring out of one of the towers of the World Trade Center. Kent told us all to leave the premises and stay home until further notice. No one knew if the JSC would be the next target.

Months flew by after 9/11 as the country slowly recovered. The work went on, but everything felt somehow different. It wasn't long before I was aware of just how much I was struggling to find my place at NASA. I still held on to my dream of traveling into space, but I was having trouble seeing how I would get there. In the wake of 9/11, everything seemed so much more important, but I couldn't find my vision. I wanted to show the world that America was the most resilient nation on the planet. You might be able to knock down one of our tallest buildings, but you could not stop us from achieving our goals. To me, NASA has always been such a central part of the American story. It is part of the dream we dared to tell about ourselves. I wanted to be part of that, to help build on that, and the struggle for me now was figuring out how.

I realized soon after that I might be able to reach my dream to travel into space by learning how to operate the robotic arm on a shuttle mission. I had my goal, and a new vision of how to get there.

I started to train obsessively in the SSTs. From there I moved on to the fixed- and motion-base training with the same laser focus. Fixed-base training is exactly what it sounds like. I was training in a stationary, simulated space shuttle with other astronauts. I worked through tasks that would train me to fly the robotic arm like it was second nature, so I could catch a satellite that was spinning out of control or grab equipment from the payload bay to attach to the space station while we were in orbit. All the while, instructors were throwing malfunctions at me, preparing me to be ready for every possible thing that could go wrong in space.

Once I mastered fixed-base training, I moved on to motion-base simulators. One simulator, the Dynamic Systems Trainer, was like playing a life-sized video game. We used hand controllers to dock and undock from the space station.

Working in the simulators was like going on the coolest ride ever at Disney World. You got to experience all the vibrations, noises, and views that astronauts would experience during an actual shuttle launch and landing. It was *almost* like taking an actual space flight. But it wasn't real. Every exercise made me realize all the more just how much I wanted to experience the real thing.

While I was training, I continued to get my hearing tested. Unfortunately, there was no further improvement. I was still hearing-impaired in my left ear. My managers at NASA wanted the best for me, but at the same time they didn't know what to do. It seemed unlikely that I would ever be physically able to leave the planet, but NASA didn't give up on me and they let me keep training.

The Canadians had developed two robotic arms for the space shuttle and the ISS, so I went to Montreal to train to fly them. Then I returned to the JSC and applied that training in the mission control center. We developed the robotic maneuvers procedures in Houston, and I tested everything in simulators to be sure it could be done safely while in orbit.

I worked with the robotics branch in Houston until September 2002, when NASA asked me to move to Washington, DC, to support the new Educator Astronaut Program (EAP). The EAP was created to get students and teachers interested in space and the space program. NASA knew that my parents were educators and that I had a passion for inspiring the next generation of explorers. I wasn't giving up the robotics branch permanently, or my hopes to fly in space. I was just on temporary loan.

Before I moved to Washington, however, I adopted a 90-pound dog named Jake. Jake was probably a mix of Rhodesian Ridgeback and Chow. He had an unpredictable nature. He could be warm and affectionate one minute and then go off and start barking up a storm the next. His behavior worried his owners, who also had a new baby. I was not looking to own a dog at that time, but five minutes after meeting Jake, I knew he was my dog. And Jake knew I was his human. Jake and I were a family.

A month later, I drove to Washington. I was going to

keep Jake with me, but I quickly realized that my travel schedule would make that too difficult to manage. My parents agreed to look after Jake in Lynchburg, and I settled for visiting him on weekends whenever I could.

EDUCATOR ASTRONAUT

The EAP program was revamped in an effort to reinvigorate the public's interest in the space program and to help recruit teachers to apply for the next astronaut candidate class. My comanager was Debbie Brown. She was the educator and I was the astronaut. People came together from across NASA to help us develop a program that we planned to kick off in January 2003. I traveled around the country talking to teachers and students about space exploration. We wanted them to think about space in a whole new light—to be excited about it. We also wanted teachers to apply to the space program, so they could teach students about space exploration in a whole new way.

At the time, I was still labeled as DNIF (Duty Not Involving Flying). At almost every stop, kids asked if I had ever flown in space. When I said no, they said I couldn't call myself a real astronaut. I'm sure the kids didn't intend to be mean—they believed that you weren't really an astronaut until you had actually been to space—but it stung every time I heard those words. It also made me more determined to find a way to make my new dream of flying into space come true.

I had been at the EAP for about four months when I decided to make a trip home to see my parents and Jake in Lynchburg. It was a Saturday morning when I left Washington, DC, to make the three-and-a-half-hour drive along the Blue Ridge Mountains. I hadn't gone far when my boss called. The shuttle *Columbia* was scheduled to land at the Kennedy Space Center in Cape Canaveral, and my boss—an educator, not an astronaut—wanted to know why the countdown clock was going up rather than down.

I immediately pulled off the highway. I knew something was wrong. Countdowns are supposed to reach zero. The shuttle should be there.

I turned on the radio and within a few minutes, I heard that NASA officials had announced that the shuttle had broken up during its reentry into Earth's atmosphere. The unthinkable had happened—again. I turned around and headed back to NASA headquarters.

Everyone at NASA HQ was focused on one thing— taking care of our families. Every astronaut chooses what's known as a crew astronaut casualty officer, or CACO, when he joins the corps. The CACO's job is to help the family interact with NASA in case of a disaster.

That afternoon I was asked to provide support to the parents of David Brown, the flight surgeon who had been among the crew. I wasn't David's CACO, but he was a close friend. David had led the investigation to find out what happened to my hearing in the NBL pool. He helped me through one of the most difficult periods of my life with a patience and grace that I'll never forget.

I drove to the home of Dorothy and Judge Paul Brown in Washington, Virginia, to help them make sense of the loss of their son. A state trooper was posted outside their home to keep the media away. I knew, and the Browns knew, that the shuttle program would come under close scrutiny and perhaps be grounded permanently.

"My son is gone; there's nothing you can do to bring him back," David's father said to me. "But the biggest tragedy would be if we don't continue to fly in space to carry on his legacy."

Judge Brown's comments, his grace in the midst of grief, hit me in the heart. I knew he was right. We couldn't give up. *I* couldn't give up. His strength and conviction in the shadow of what I know was one of the darkest moments of his life changed how I felt about my place in this world and gave me a whole new understanding of what it means to think of others first. In that moment, I dedicated myself to doing everything I could to honor his words.

The next Monday I attended a staff meeting of everyone in the EAP. I was exhausted and emotionally spent from the sudden loss of my seven friends. In Houston, astronauts were briefed and offered medical and psychiatric care if needed. The *Columbia* crew were family members, but as the only astronaut traveling in the EAP, I felt as if I was on an island. I felt that no one around me understood how I felt or what it meant to have seven of your buddies, your family, die all at once, in a flash, for the whole world to see.

What happened to the shuttle to make it explode on reentry? As it turns out, a piece of foam insulation had broken off the side of the *Columbia* and hit the left wing eighty seconds after its launch from Cape Canaveral. The shuttle lost a portion of a protective tile, and that damage went undetected. When the shuttle attempted to reenter Earth's atmosphere two weeks later, intense heat entered the damaged left wing and tore it apart.

As I suspected, the *Columbia* tragedy meant the shuttle program was grounded indefinitely. Nobody seemed to know what would happen. The five shuttles had flown 111 successful missions, but we knew the two disasters would shape the shuttle's story in the mind of the public forever.

The sudden uncertainty surrounding the space program coincided with my own uncertainty about my future. As I was dealing with the loss of my friends, I was also dealing with the growing realization I would always be hearing impaired.

A few days later, President George W. Bush arrived at the Johnson Space Center to deliver a memorial speech in honor of the *Columbia* crew. I wasn't there to hear him in person, but his words still moved me.

"Our whole nation was blessed to have such men and women serving in our space program," he said. "Their loss is deeply felt, especially in this place, where so many of you called them friends. The people of NASA are being tested once again. In your grief, you are responding as your friends would have wished—with focus, professionalism, and unbroken faith in the mission of this agency."

He went on to proclaim that the space program would go on. "This cause of exploration and discovery is not an option we choose; it is a desire written in the human heart," he told the gathered mourners. "We are that part of creation which seeks to understand all creation. We find the best among us, send them forth into unmapped darkness, and pray they will return. They go in peace for all mankind, and all mankind is in their debt."

His words resonated with me and gave me hope. Maybe this wouldn't be the end of space exploration. Maybe I would still have a chance to fulfill my dreams of looking down on Mother Earth.

What I didn't know then was the huge toll it was all taking on me. Since the shuttle explosion, I'd spent nearly every free minute helping the families of the crew members. I didn't allow myself to mourn the loss of my friends. I didn't allow myself to cry at the memorials. I felt that my crying wouldn't help anyone. I had been in caregiver mode—but nobody was caring for me.

Several weeks went by before I flew to Houston for the first time since the accident. I will never forget the feeling as I turned my car onto NASA Parkway and headed toward the entrance of the space center. On the side of the road, in front of the sign that read "Lyndon B. Johnson Space Center," were hundreds, perhaps thousands, of bouquets of flowers, letters, prayers, Bibles, and American flags. It was a spontaneous, and utterly heartfelt, memorial.

I pulled my car over and, for the first time, I cried. I really, really cried. Not just for the crew that was lost but for myself, too, a broken, grounded, dreamless astronaut.

It didn't register at the time, but it turned out the agency's chief flight surgeon, Dr. Richard Williams, had been watching me closely as we flew from town to town to see the families and attend the memorial services. I'd noticed him taking notes on takeoffs and landings, but I didn't know what for. It turned out he was assessing my ears and how I handled the changes in air pressure during flight. I could only really hear out of one ear since the incident, but other than that, I felt fine.

A few weeks after the last memorial, Williams summoned me to his office at NASA headquarters. I had no idea why he wanted to see me, but when I walked into his office, he stood and extended his hand to me.

"Leland," he said, "I'm going to sign a waiver so you can fly to space."

CHAPTER 11

TRAINING FOR SPACE

I was finally going to get a chance to fly in space! I couldn't help but think of Jeannette's prophecy and marvel that it had come to pass. I called my dear childhood friend Mary Gordon, who had supported me throughout my NASA career, and told her the news. I think she was even more excited than I was because she saw it as an affirmation of faith. Persistence, prayer, and belief in yourself can indeed make great things happen.

Soon after that conversation I realized I had done all I could in the Educator Astronaut Program. We had succeeded in getting kids and teachers excited about the space program. A number of teachers we met had decided to apply to become astronauts, and our top choices would be moving on to the selection process in Houston. It was time for me to head back to Houston to be part of that final process.

In late May, I picked up Jake in Lynchburg and continued south to my home in El Lago, Texas. But we didn't stay long. A couple of weeks later, Jake and I hit the road. I wanted to take a vacation before training started again. Jake and I visited the Grand Canyon, Hoover Dam, and Yosemite National Park. We camped out and took in the natural environment. In Yosemite, a beautiful wilderness area characterized by granite cliffs, waterfalls, clear streams, and giant sequoia groves, we sat by a campfire and I stared up at the night sky to see how many constellations I could name—the twins Castor and Pollux, Orion's Rigel and Betelgeuse. One night Jake woke me, trying to get out of the tent by opening the zipper with his nose. For once he wasn't barking. He was too busy trying to protect me from a bear that had wandered into camp!

Park rangers told us the next morning that a bear had been stealing improperly stored food and had broken into some cars with food in them. I was glad that Jake was smart enough to stay silent and that I was smart enough to keep him inside. We both could have been bear food.

In September 2003, I returned from my vacation back to the hustle and bustle of Houston. In addition to training,

I was asked to serve on the astronaut selection committee. I was now on the other side of the table, listening to why applicants thought they had the right stuff to join the astronaut corps. I couldn't believe how accomplished some of the candidates were—multiple PhDs, advanced pilot and scuba qualifications, and one had even hiked ten of the world's ninety-six fourteeners (mountains that have peaks with an elevation of at least 14,000 feet).

I spent much of 2004 on the road while I waited for a flight assignment. The year began with a trip to Washington, DC, in January to serve as what I called an "Astronaut Potted Plant." My job was to smile and nod while President George W. Bush talked about the future of the space program.

President Bush charted a course for future missions, including the development of a new human space vehicle and a return to the moon. "With the experience and knowledge gained on the moon," he said, "we will then be ready to take the next steps of space exploration: human missions to Mars and to worlds beyond."

Since its founding in 1958, NASA has pushed the boundaries of human spaceflight, space science, and aeronautics. The work done at NASA not only changed the way we build and fly airplanes and space vehicles, it also dramatically changed humans' understanding of the universe and our own planet. I hoped to play a small part in furthering that understanding—but first I needed an actual mission assignment!

My NASA work picked up again at the end of 2004 and into 2005. In January 2005, fellow astronaut John Herrington and I met with students, teachers, and education officials in remote villages in Alaska to talk about the space program. That summer, instead of palling around with Jake, I began kayak training in Palmer, Alaska, with astronauts Jim Halsell, TJ Creamer, Paolo Nespoli, Terry Virts, and Robert Thirsk. We traveled by boat to Prince William Sound and were dropped off on a small tidal island near Nassau Fjord. As with all NASA wilderness trips, we were being evaluated for our ability to be part of an ISS expedition. The skills learned there—expedition behavior, planning, decision-making, wilderness medicine, communication, cooking, self-care, team care, leadership, and followership—were all very applicable, and essential, to space travel and to functioning at the high level that's expected of all astronauts on a mission. The trip was about more than just learning to kayak—no one would be kayaking in space. It was about learning to be part of a group and showing that you could do what needed to be done to survive without the trappings of civilization around. Can you respond calmly and effectively to any new situation, no matter how surprising or scary?

One day I took the lead position in our kayak. The

water was turbulent. A storm was brewing, and I had to decide if we could reach our destination before the rain hit or if we needed to choose a closer, secondary place to put in for the night. Once the decision was made to go for our original target, it was my responsibility to keep everyone on the team safe and together. I was one of the stronger rowers and made sure I did not pull too far ahead of the group. Making sure the whole team got to shore safely was the most important part of my job as a leader.

At the same time, I started to think about life *after* NASA, and realized that I would one day return to Virginia. I had talked to my dad about getting a few acres in the country to build on. One day my dad called and told me he had bumped into a man who happened to have some land he wanted to sell in nearby Appomattox, Virginia, where the Civil War ended. I flew to Lynchburg and walked the fields, marveling that this was the place where Union or Confederate soldiers had probably camped out nearly 150 years ago. My dad and I both liked what we saw, and in July 2006, we closed the deal. It was so peaceful there. Huge clouds meandered across the sky, casting shadows on the serene fields. That image stayed with me and inspired me to name the farm Serenity.

My 90 acres were half wooded and half soybean fields, crisscrossed by streams. Fox, deer, and bear tracks peppered the property. There was an old tobacco barn and a log cabin.

I continued to live in Houston and only got to Lynchburg on holidays, but on each trip I took the time to visit Serenity. My work with the EAP and in STEAM (Science, Technology, Engineering, Arts, and Mathematics) education had led me to believe that in order to appreciate the wonders of the natural world, kids need to do hands-on projects. I began to envision a camp on the property as a way to enable kids to connect with nature while learning about science, engineering, and technology.

A huge oak tree on the property helped me to visualize my dream and inspired me to write the following poem:

Serenity Tree
He sits there boldly, proudly, protecting all he sees
Much girth, but more height with a crown made of leaves
Green hues flutter lazy, in the summer breeze
While he watches all the want-to-be emboldened little trees
The land can sleep soundly while Serenity stands guard.
Bear, fox, and cougars come to stalk and prowl the yard.
He stands above the swaying grass, the flower tree in bloom.
He also sees the gurgling brook lit softly by the moon.
He watches butterflies fly and honeybees buzz. They keep
doing what they do really just because.
He's endured winter storms and brutal sweltering heat.

Infestations of locust and a neighing horse's beat.
He saw brother against brother in an uncivilized war.
Bodies strewn about him like he'd never seen before.
Serenity for countless years has stood strong and fast. Just like Serenity Farm will tell rich stories while many years pass.

The idea of serenity fit in well with my general even-keeled demeanor and my faith. I often consulted 2 Timothy 1:7. "For God has not given us a spirit of fear and timidity, but of power, love, and self-discipline."

I believed, as I headed back to astronaut training in Houston, that living a life of faith would prepare me for the moment when I would finally soar into space.

It's been said that astronauts are always training, even when they don't have a specific mission. And that's absolutely true, but once you're assigned to a flight, things get real serious real fast. For every one hour in space, an astronaut has to spend at least one hundred hours training on land. There's no room for error when you're orbiting Earth at 17,500 miles per hour. We have to be ready for anything—solar flares, orbital debris, suit leaks, loss of communication with the ground, or even the potential for a possible alien encounter.

Even though I'd been waiting for what seemed like

forever for my chance, when Kent Rominger, chief of the astronaut office, called and told me I was going to space, the news seemed to arrive totally out of the blue. I was assigned to mission STS-122 under the command of Stephen Frick. My fellow mission specialists were Stan Love and Rex J. Walheim, along with Hans Schlegel and Léopold Eyharts, two astronauts from the European Space Agency (ESA). Alan "Dex" Poindexter would be our pilot. I was at home in Houston when the call came, and I remember jumping in the air and letting out a loud scream, pumping my fists and saying, "Yes!" Jake was the first to know I'd gotten my chance. He woke up, wondering what in the world was going on. I got down on the floor and hugged him before I called my folks.

PREPARING TO LAUNCH

The projected launch date for STS-122 was December 2007, which gave us almost a year and a half to train and prepare. Our mission was to deliver the ESA's two-billion-dollar Columbus Laboratory to the International Space Station. The ESA regarded the Columbus as its future center of activities in space and had been waiting ten years to have the 23-by-15-foot research laboratory installed.

My job would be to connect the Columbus lab to the ISS using the robotic arm. I recall walking into a meeting not long after the mission crew was announced and hearing our flight director introduce me by saying, "This is STS-122 mission specialist Leland Melvin. He is going to install the Columbus," and marveling as the room burst into applause.

I felt tremendous gratitude but also so much pressure knowing that the ESA had been waiting so long for this moment. A European flight controller, one of the project leaders, turned to me as I was walking out of the room, and in a thick German accent said, "Don't screw it up."

Training requirements for a mission are laid out almost a year in advance. For my first flight, most of the training took place in Houston, where the fixed- and motion-base space shuttle simulators are located. I practiced flying both shuttle and station robotic arms over and over again so that when I was in space, the steps would be second nature.

But, man, it wasn't easy. I remember once when I was training on the Dynamic Systems Trainer and I nearly killed everyone on the simulated space shuttle. I was using the hand controllers to maneuver the space station's robotic arm into the shuttle's payload bay to grasp the Columbus Lab and get it ready to attach to the space station. As I maneuvered the robotic arm, I lost my situational awareness for a moment and didn't realize that the arm's elbow was swinging toward the shuttle. And the next thing I knew, the elbow smashed into the shuttle. Had that happened for real, in space, anyone on the shuttle would have had just seconds to get from the shuttle onto the space station and to close the hatches. More than a few seconds and the whole station would have lost pressure and the whole crew would have died.

Yep, I messed up—but that's why we train so hard before we fly into space. Mistakes on Earth are learning opportunities; mistakes in space are deadly.

The facilities in Houston also included a virtual reality (VR) lab. While I executed the robotics operations, the EVA astronauts, Rex , Stan, and Hans, donned VR goggles, gloves, and portable life support systems, to immerse themselves in the world of virtual spacewalks. They "virtually" worked beside me while I "virtually" installed the Columbus Lab to the outside of the space station.

One of the coolest training sessions involved both EVA and robotics. In the Neutral Buoyancy Laboratory, the same place where I'd nearly lost my hearing more than five years earlier, we practiced reach and feel with objects that were the actual size of the lab so we could make sure the interfaces between human and machine were reproduced properly in a situation as close to the real one as we could re-create.

I would sit outside the pool and operate the robotic arms in the control room, while the EVA astronauts did their "spacewalks" submerged in the water. It was essential that we had the opportunity to practice maneuvers in a situation as close to the space station structure as possible, because if we did one step incorrectly, someone could die. The robotic arm could easily crush an astronaut or, my worst nightmare, break their glass visors, suffocating them instantly in the void of space.

All this was why it was critically important for the space walkers to give me clear directions regarding where they wanted to travel and the distance they wanted to go. It took weeks of training, but eventually I knew the exact location they needed to be to perform specific tasks. The space walker has a limited operational envelope or radius to reach, turn, and grab items while attached to the arm. They had to trust that I was using the space shuttle and station cameras to monitor clearances between the hardware and their bodies to ensure no collisions would occur. If anything looked unsafe, it was my job to say "Stop motion" and to reassess the situation. Nothing takes a backseat to safety.

I loved flying the robotic arm. When I was in the zone, it was almost like being back on the football field. The training just took over. I could manipulate the hand controllers to make the arm move through space with the grace of a dancer.

Other training took place off-site. In October of 2006, I joined Steve, Alan, Rex, Hans, and Stan for a survival training course in Canyonlands, Utah. The road and trails had been washed out by the kind of flood that only happens once every one hundred years. So instead of being bused to our campground, we had to hike ten miles with our 85-pound backpacks. And that was before our two-week survival training course even started.

Our instructors pushed us to our limits to see how we reacted as a team in a variety of conditions. We experienced everything from warm sunlit days in the canyon to rain to hiking over snow-covered rocks.

As we hiked from White Canyon into Long Canyon, we added rappelling, using ropes to help us make our way down a steep rock face, and rock climbing to our list of skills.

One of the most difficult days was when we had to ford a river with our heavy backpacks. The water was high and moving fast because of the previous weeks' flooding. I was about halfway across when I found myself stuck in quick mud—a kind of quicksand found in river bottoms. As a wide receiver, I was used to running fast and moving my feet quickly. That's exactly the wrong thing to do when you're trapped in quick mud. The faster you try to move, the faster you sink. Everyone around me was in the same predicament, so we couldn't help one another. (The trick, I learned later, is to pull your feet out of the mud very, very slowly. The faster you pull, the more you create a vacuum around your foot and get stuck even more.)

It might seem strange to say, but trying to get myself out of that mud was one of the hardest things I had to do in all my astronaut training. More than once I thought I was going to drown. At one point, an uprooted tree came careering at me. It took all my strength to get out of its way in time. I took my pack off and tried to throw it toward the shore. Bad idea. Our instructor, Chris, managed to grab it, or I would have been without my food and gear for the rest of the trip.

All of this was in preparation for the space shuttle and space station, for space itself. Getting to know one another, and our own limits, ahead of time could save lives in space. I learned, for instance, that when Alan "Dex" Poindexter got irritable, that often meant he was thirsty and I'd better find him something to drink. And when I get tired, I get quiet. That was important information for me and my crewmates to have if we were going to be successful in space.

The following spring I headed to Memorial Hermann-Texas Medical Center in Houston to learn the basics of emergency medicine.

Every space shuttle mission has a designated medical officer. Often it just so happens that one of the astronauts on a mission is a medical doctor. We had no such person on my first shuttle flight, so I volunteered to take on the task.

The medical officer is responsible for handling any medical problems and emergencies that come up during the mission, along with routine stuff like handing out medicine to help with congestion, irritable stomachs, or even just to help people sleep. Sleeping in microgravity—floating in your sleeping bag while you're tethered to a wall—can be difficult when you're not used to it, and it's important to get a good night's rest, especially if you are performing a strenuous spacewalk the next day.

The medical training took eight weeks and covered everything from stitching up wounds to giving injections. I was assigned to work with Dr. Red Duke. He had been a young surgical resident at Dallas's Parkland Memorial Hospital on November 22, 1963, when President John F. Kennedy was shot and killed by Lee Harvey Oswald. Dr. Duke was the first doctor on hand to receive the president before he had to turn his attention to saving the life of another patient brought in that afternoon. Though he didn't realize it immediately, that other patient was John Connally, the Texas governor who also took a bullet that day but survived.

Dr. Duke was famous not only for his skills in the operating room and in trauma medicine, but also for his folksy, country-doctor manner. He liked to hum Willie Nelson songs around the emergency room. Congressman Ted Poe once described him as "John Wayne in scrubs."

Luckily for NASA, Dr. Duke was also a huge fan of the space program.

On my first day training in the ER, a teenage boy was wheeled in with a large gash on his leg, the result of a car accident. "Go stitch him up, Leland," Dr. Duke shouted. The cut was several inches long, and the first step was to stitch the muscle underneath, something I had not practiced. If there's one thing they teach you in the astronaut corps, it is how to act confident in the face of uncertainty.

"How many of these have you done?" I remember the boy asking me, his big eyes staring into mine.

"Enough," I responded in my reassuring, positive voice. I had practiced on mannequins and cadavers. He didn't need to know that I had never worked on a living person.

Later that same day, I inserted a tube into a man's stomach through his nose, also a first. But perhaps my most dramatic trial came when a young woman was wheeled into the ER. She had been the driver in a collision that had killed her friend. We needed to insert an IV, but her veins had collapsed. A rattled young resident was having no success inserting the needle into her jugular vein in her neck, the only accessible artery.

"Leland, take over," Dr. Duke said.

I pulled on a set of sterile gloves, took the needle from the resident, and with a steady hand, inserted it into the vein in one try. I knew I had to do it, and I did. My hands didn't shake until I was done! My success earned me an instant reputation in the ER as someone who could get things done.

Our scheduled flight date was pushed from December 2007 until February 2008 due to an engine-cutoff sensor problem. There were four sensors that measured the fuel level in the big orange external tank that weren't working. If we operated the pumps inside the three main engines without fuel, the engines could blow apart, damaging the vehicle and killing all of us. So you could say those sensors were pretty essential. We had to move the *Atlantis* from the launchpad back to the vehicle assembly building to get the sensors changed out for new ones. We all headed back to Houston. After waiting so long for a flight, I was frustrated with the delay.

Finally, they scheduled our launch. But before we could head to Cape Canaveral for final preparations, we were isolated in JSC crew quarters in Houston for a week. Visitors had to be cleared by a doctor because no one wanted to take any germs into space. Our families weren't with us, but our nonhuman robotic simulators were, so to pass the time, we practiced and practiced and practiced until we finally flew to Cape Canaveral for the final five days of prep before launch.

Launch day was slated for February 7, 2008. I

remember every moment of it. I remember walking out of the astronaut crew quarters and coming down the elevator. I remember how when the doors opened there were lights and cameras and our friends and family members who had come to cheer us on. I remember that my high school chemistry teacher, Cornelea Campbell, and her son Cornel were among those on hand; I remember hearing Cornel yell my name so loud that everyone heard it. We stopped and waved to the jubilant crowd as we boarded the Astro Van, a modified airstream camper, and made our way to the launchpad.

On the ride to the launchpad, I thought about the long journey that had brought me to this point. Typically, an astronaut will be assigned to a mission after basic shuttle and station training, which takes about a year and a half. Because of my medical situation, my path was far from typical: I had trained for this for nearly ten years.

In the van I looked over at Rex, whom I would be sitting next to in the space shuttle. We exchanged grins. Finally, it was our turn. I was going to space.

CHAPTER 12
THE FINAL FRONTIER

We climbed into the space shuttle *Atlantis* and strapped in according to seat order. Dex and Steve, the pilot and commander, went first, then Rex and I were seated on the flight deck. We were followed by Stan, Leo, and Hans, who all sat on the mid-deck below us. Suit techs and astronaut support personnel made sure we didn't bump into any of the switches and equipment while we were getting in. Once we were connected to oxygen and to the "chiller" that would keep us cool in our suits over the next three hours, we did a suit check to make sure we had no leaks. The checklists, notepads, and pens we needed on flight were tethered to our suits so that they wouldn't float away when we reached space.

A few minutes before launch, I fist-bumped with Dex, Steve, and Rex. The safety systems were armed and the balance and pressure systems were checked.

The countdown began.

Six seconds prior to liftoff, the main engines came to life. The thrust from them tilted the entire shuttle stack slowly forward and then back again. NASA folks call this the "twang" because, like a door spring used to stop a door from hitting the wall, it makes that sound as it bends back and forth.

Next, thousands of gallons of water were activated from a tank just above the launchpad. The sound of the solid rocket boosters is loud enough to completely shatter the concrete-and-steel launching pad. The deluge of water floods everything below the shuttle and suppresses the force of the sound.

Then there was the thunderous roar of the solid rocket boosters coming to life.

And we were off.

Imagine you're in a fast sports car going about 100 miles per hour. Our acceleration was 100,000 times more intense. We were pinned in our seats, feeling three times our weight on our chests as we penetrated the sound barrier. I remember laboring to breathe a bit for about two minutes until we used up the solid rocket boosters and jettisoned them. The load got a little lighter and my breathing got easier.

We were heading to space.

About a minute later, we were traveling 10,000 miles per hour over the east coast of the US, the Atlantic Ocean sparkling in the background. It only took eight and a half minutes to reach our optimal speed of 17,500 miles per hour. We were in orbit and going fast enough to shut down the engines and jettison the now-empty external fuel tank.

Each member of a shuttle crew is allowed to carry mementos to space.

My personal items included two NFL jerseys (the Lions and the Cowboys, of course), a beloved Curious George book from my childhood, jazz bassist Christian McBride's *Live at Tonic* album, and recordings of some songs I had composed myself in my little home studio. Among my mementos was a work of art created by youngsters at Project Row Houses (PRH). Based in one of the oldest African-American neighborhoods in Houston, PRH aims to use art to transform the social environment. I had visited the PRH Arts/Education Program and talked to the children about my upcoming shuttle mission. Nearly fifty neighborhood youngsters, all between the ages of five and fourteen, created a 3-by-5-foot quilt reflecting what space meant to them. They worked all that summer to complete it, and I took it up with me into the cosmos.

As soon as the engines shut down, it was time for my first on-orbit task. Hans and I unstrapped from our seats to take images of the fuel tank as it plunged toward the Indian Ocean. I recorded video and he shot still images, making sure there were no holes in the Spray-On Foam Insulation (SOFI) that covered the tank. The SOFI helps keep engine fuel, liquid oxygen, and hydrogen from boiling away. If we saw missing foam, it was possible that it could have hit and damaged the fragile tiles that covered the wings and orbiter belly.

From space, our views of Earth's bodies of water—with all their various shades and pigments—would challenge even a painter's vocabulary. There aren't enough words to describe all the shades of blue in the Caribbean Sea alone.

But we weren't up there merely to admire Earth. As soon as we were safely in orbit, we set about converting the shuttle from a rocket ship into our home away from home. We would be living in it for three days until we reached the space station. Helmets and gloves came off and we got busy setting up the kitchen galley and toilet. We also had to reconfigure the computers from launch mode to the on-orbit mode.

Atlantis is named after R/V *Atlantis*, a two-masted sailing ship that served as a research vessel for the Woods Hole Oceanographic Institution from 1930 to 1966. Like the sailing ship, *Atlantis* charted new territory to further our understanding of the world.

There are two parts to the crew cabin in the space shuttle: the mid-deck, where we live, eat, sleep, wash, and go to the bathroom; and the flight deck, where the windows and flight controls are. The mid-deck is about the size of a large walk-in closet, which is pretty small for seven adults. We made it work for the three days it was our home. Because in space, unlike on the ground, you can float up and use every square inch of that space—you can hang out on the ceiling!

Once we had accomplished our initial task of turning the shuttle into our home, we opened the payload doors and activated the shuttle's robotic arm to make sure nothing had happened to damage the arm during launch. I had been training to operate the device for almost two years. It was a joy to finally use it in space.

We were too busy for me to really think about what it was like to live in space—having to chase after your food while it floated past you, floating in a sleeping bag while tethered to the wall, and the difficulty of going to the bathroom without gravity. I would be on the space station before I really was able to step back to marvel at the experience of all of those things.

On flight day two, our first full day in orbit, we flew the arm to grapple, or take hold of, our inspection boom. Moving the boom, we scanned the orbiter to make sure our heat shields hadn't been damaged on ascent. All was well. We also started preparing for the first of the three spacewalks that would take place after we connected with the ISS.

We began flight day three about 40 miles behind the space station, checking off the steps in our rendezvous procedures and using laptops, a laser ranger, and cameras to get in the right position below and just ahead of the station. Then we had to be in exactly the right spot to let it "catch" us while both vehicles were flying at a speed of 17,500 miles per hour, orbiting around Earth every ninety minutes.

A series of coordinated Orbital Maneuvering System (OMS) engine burns got us closer to the space station. Our next task was to "contact and capture" the International Space Station. A docking/berthing connection is referred to as either "soft" or "hard." First we initiated *soft dock* by making contact with the ISS and latching our docking connector to the space station's. Once we knew that soft connection was secure, and both spacecraft were pressurized, we moved on to the *hard dock*. At the moment of hard dock, both the shuttle and the ISS are tightly sealed together.

With that done, we joined Steve, our commander, in a brief celebration of our safe rendezvous. Then we worked through a variety of leak check procedures. Leaks in space are deadly. Leaks mean depressurization and a complete loss of oxygen. Without oxygen, of course, there can be no human life. As soon as we were sure there were no leaks, we knew it would be safe to open the hatches between the space shuttle and space station.

In 1998, the first two modules of the International Space Station had been launched and joined together in orbit. Space shuttle missions like mine brought more modules—mostly research laboratories—and the first crew arrived in 2000. Today the station is essentially a football field–sized series of interlocking units. Once in operation, the Columbus module we carried would be used to conduct biology experiments on microorganisms, cells, small plants, and even small invertebrates like insects to learn about the effects of microgravity and space radiation on biological organisms.

Station commander Peggy Whitson and her crew, Yuri Malenchenko and Dan Tani, were happy to see us. When you spend months away from home with only a few other people, new faces are always welcome. Peggy and Yuri were four months into a six-month mission. Dan would be heading home with us on our return flight and Leo would be replacing him on the station.

Most of the modules on the station have four sides, just like a room on Earth. In space, when you're floating in microgravity, you don't really have an up and a down. The rooms are put together in a way that enables the crew to work continuously on flat planes, either on a wall, a floor, another wall, or what we think of as the ceiling. Handrails, tethers, Velcro, and other devices keep objects, and sometimes humans, securely attached to the work surfaces so nothing floats away in the middle of a task.

In addition to the workspaces, there is a kitchen and two bathrooms on the station. Learning to go to the bathroom in space is something we didn't train for much on the ground, and it definitely took some getting used to. The bathrooms are tiny and have a very small toilet with an opening about the same size as a jar of spaghetti sauce for solid waste. A hose topped with a yellow funnel is for liquid waste.

In space *everything* floats, and you definitely don't want that to include what really belongs in the toilet. Foot restraints help you stay in place, and vacuum suction moves waste away from your body into storage compartments. There are systems on board to purify liquid waste and turn it into drinking water. (Yes, in space we drink our urine.)

Solid waste gets sucked into a bag that sits inside a metal can. Once the can is full, it's sealed and put into a trash module. As trash modules are filled, they're let go into space. The trash modules gradually fall to Earth and burn up as they enter the atmosphere.

Sleeping quarters on the station are almost as small as the bathrooms. Each sleep station is a bit bigger than a sleeping bag, with just enough room for a computer and a few books. We strapped our sleeping bags to the wall with bungees and floated in place while we slept.

Our real mission began with a spacewalk on day five to begin attaching the Columbus Lab to the space station. Before passing through an airlock and a hatch to enter the vacuum of space, Rex and Stan put on suits with bulky backpacks that housed everything from oxygen, heating, cooling, and carbon dioxide removal systems to a high-powered computer, all of which would have weighed about 300 pounds on Earth. But in space they were next to weightless.

Once out in space, Stan attached a grapple fixture to Columbus, which enabled me to grab the roughly 5,000-pound lab with the 58-foot robotic arm and pull it out of the shuttle's payload bay. With Dan and Leo at the robotics workstation, I kept a close eye on the monitors while I used the arm to maneuver the 23-by-15-foot shiny module into place. It required a lot of careful configuration and constant reconfiguration to line it up with the station just right.

We had beautiful views of Earth through the monitors as we pulled Columbus into its berth on the outside of the space station. Our space walkers made sure everything was connected properly from the outside. I remembered the voice of the German flight controller telling me, "Don't screw it up" when we first met back in Houston two years before the flight.

The spacewalk took seven hours and fifty-eight minutes. I call that a good day's work.

While we slept, flight control conducted a variety of leak checks, and on flight day six, we were given the go-ahead to open the hatches between the station and the Columbus Lab. We powered up computers, power distribution units, and heaters. By afternoon, circulation fans had cleaned out dust and other particulates from the air, and we were able to go in and out of the new lab to hook up water, thermal controls, and command and monitoring units.

Our second and third spacewalks on flight days seven and nine involved more work with the Columbus, including attaching an external telescope, switching out a nitrogen tank on the space station, and retrieving a broken gyroscope for repair and reuse. On these procedures, I operated the robotic arm, making sure we did our work carefully, quickly, and perfectly.

There are so many unforgettable aspects of life in space, including the experiments, the robotics, and the spacewalks, but I think my most memorable moment took place when Peggy and her crew invited us to have dinner over in the Russian service module.

When you have a list of tasks to accomplish in a short amount of time like we did, we ate when we could. And of course the space shuttle and the space station each had their own food supplies. But on the day that the Columbus Lab was successfully installed, we had a dinner to celebrate.

"You guys bring the vegetables, we'll bring the meat," Peggy said.

We gathered around a small table. Some of us were floating above it and others below. We were French, German, Russian, Asian-American, and African-American, listening to music by the singer Sade and having a meal in space. We were orbiting around the planet every 90 minutes at 17,500 mph. There were sunsets and sunrises every 45 minutes, and out the window we could see every place on the planet, from Afghanistan to Antarctica.

Two hundred and forty miles above the Earth, I sat in peace with people we had once counted among our nation's enemies. Here we were bound by a common commitment to explore space for the benefit of all humanity. It was one of those amazing moments when you realize just how much we can accomplish when we all work together. It was one of the most inspiring moments of my life.

While the celebration with Peggy's crew included Russian and international cuisine along with canned beef and barley, most of our space meals consisted of typical American fare. Many people associate astronaut food with that freeze-dried ice cream you can buy in museum gift shops. In truth, you won't find that on the space station, but you will find thermally stabilized and irradiated food that tastes a lot like the same foods served on Earth. People expect it to taste terrible, but it's actually pretty good.

Some dishes need only to be heated, while others require the addition of water first. My favorite space foods included beef brisket, mac and cheese, and string beans with almonds. M&M's and Raisinets made great snacks, with the added bonus of being fun to play with in space. We trapped the tiny treats in water bubbles and as the water bubbles floated by, we slurped them up.

Without gravity, food and drink moves more slowly through your digestive system, so you feel fuller for a longer period of time. It's also true that food has less taste in space, though we don't know why. The ISS food pantry is filled with things like ketchup, mustard, and hot sauce to make up for the blah factor.

Staying properly nourished and fit was critical to our

Me wearing my Detroit Lions football jersey in space during STS-122, 2008.

Making history! The first time two African-American men (me and Bobby Satcher) were in space together.

Hanging out with Neil deGrasse Tyson, Washington, DC.

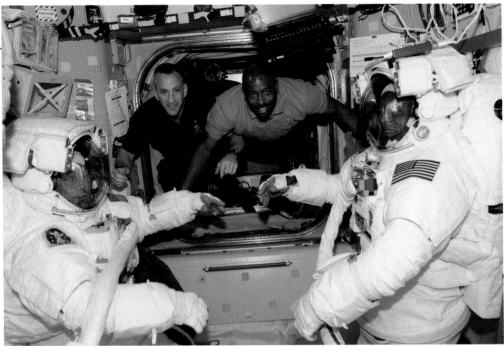

Shuttle Commander Charlie "Scorch" Hobaugh and I help mission specialist Bobby Satcher and Mike Foreman get ready for their space walk!

Mom, dad, Cathy, and Britt (Cathy's daughter) came with me into space in 2

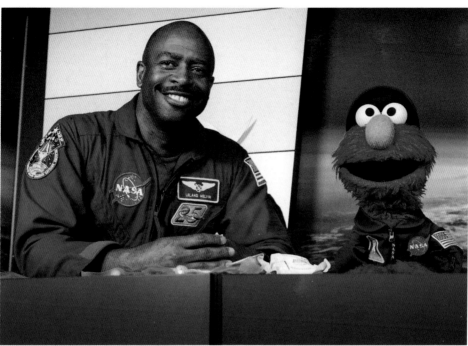

Teaching Elmo how to stay clean in space at the Kennedy Space Center, 2011.

Me at NASA's Black History Month program in Washington, DC, honoring Dr. George Carruthers and Dr. Katherine Johnson for their stellar contributions to NASA, 2016.

With two of my fellow BattleBots *judges, Fon Davis and Jessica Chobot.*

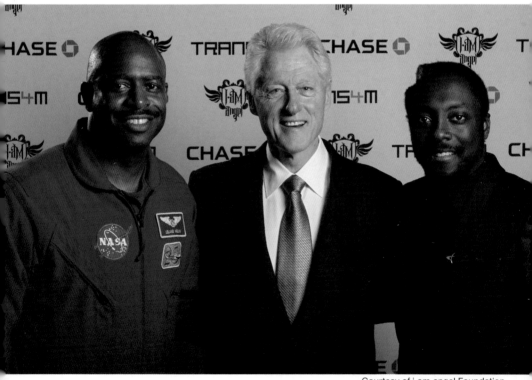

Posing with President Bill Clinton and will.i.am.

Honoring Katherine Johnson, a NASA legend and trailblazer.

Pharrell Williams and I present music legend Quincy Jones with my space montage at a ceremony in Washington, DC, 2008.

Astronaut Ron Garan, astronaut Anousheh Ansari, Bill Nye, and me at the Global Citizen Festival in New York City, 2016.

Speaking to young girls about space.

Courtesy of NASA

(From left to right) United States Chief Technology Officer Megan Smith, Canadian astronaut Chris Hadfield, NASA astronaut Stephanie Wilson, author Margot Lee Shetterly, NASA Deputy Administrator Dava Newman, NASA astronaut Yvonne Cagle, and I arrive on the red carpet at the SVA Theatre in New York for the celebration of the film Hidden Figures, *Saturday, Dec. 10, 2016.*

Hardware in space.

A shot of the STS-129 launch.

Beautiful blue Caribbean waters from space, 2009.

success at performing the jobs we had to do. Without the pressure of gravity, the body begins to do funky things. For example, every vertebra feels free to move, stretching the spine. I'm five foot eleven on Earth but I was six feet tall on the ISS. After my spine elongated, when I went to bed on the first night I felt some pains in my lower back. I had to curl up in a ball to alleviate the discomfort. The heart also changes in space. It gets smaller and changes shape because it doesn't have to pump as hard to pull the blood up from your feet. Without gravity, our bones change, too. They lose calcium and become more brittle. As a preventive measure, the ISS crew members worked out on a treadmill specially designed to help us combat loss of bone density. Some astronauts even experience pressure changes in their skulls that change the shape of their eyeballs, requiring them to wear glasses in space. We kept different prescriptions of glasses on board just in case someone's vision changed. Luckily, that didn't happen to me.

I saw so many amazing things from the vantage point of space, but a few images really took my breath away. There was the green glow we saw from above the southern hemisphere that was so different from the purple and yellow and blue lights from above the northern hemisphere—all of which was caused by particles hitting the atmosphere. I had been warned that cosmic rays would pass through the vehicle and hit my optic nerves and make me think I was seeing flashes of light that weren't there. The flashes seemed like sunbursts; colors exploded unexpectedly right before my eyes. It was crazy and beautiful and unlike anything I'd experienced before or since.

Sleep brought a different kind of light show. It was a pretty incredible experience in itself because in space you don't really have the sensation of lying down. We floated inside our sleeping bags as we dozed amid a din of pumps and motors that made sounds like we were in the middle of a factory. My dreams were more vivid than they ever had been on Earth. The colors behind my closed lids intertwined with my dream state. I sometimes saw green clusters of light moving and dancing in a way that made me think of alien forms, of little green men on Mars. At one point in the mission, a huge, In-N-Out cheeseburger, dripping with grease, began to float through my dreams. I was chomping on that burger like I didn't want to miss a single morsel. I guess the irradiated food I'd had for dinner that night wasn't very satisfying.

There was no birthday cake on the shuttle, but that didn't stop me from celebrating my own big day on February 15, flight day nine. The astronaut family support office brought my parents, sister, and a host of friends to a conference room at NASA Langley for a surprise party. Through a video hookup I saw all their beaming faces, surrounded by blue balloons and noisemakers, as they gathered around a cake. My parents wore gray sweatshirts with "Atlantis" emblazoned across the front. I had just finished a long, challenging day operating the arm, and seeing their faces made me happier than they possibly could have realized.

"A lot of prayers are going up to you," my dad told me.

"A lot of prayers are coming down to you," I replied.

The "party" ended with the whole group serenading me. Rudy King, a coworker at NASA Langley who often played basketball with me, blew out the candle.

"This is really special, guys," I said. "If I cried, the tears would just float away. So I'll save the tears for when I get home."

Two days later, on flight day eleven, we had one last meal with the ISS crew. Then they raided our food supplies to add variety to their own stores before the hatches between *Atlantis* and the ISS were closed. The next morning *Atlantis* undocked from the ISS, and like that, we were on our way home.

We did one last 360-degree fly-around of the station before beginning a de-orbit burn. Reentry into Earth's atmosphere is one of the biggest challenges of spaceflight. If the shuttle's angle is too steep relative to the atmosphere, too much heat is generated and the spacecraft burns up along with everyone inside. If the angle is too shallow, the spacecraft skims off the edge of the atmosphere like a stone skimming along the surface of a pond. The ideal reentry trajectory is a narrow band between those two extremes. Our shuttle pilot and commander got it just right. We started to bleed off the enormous speed we'd attained when the rocket boosters had sent us hurtling from the pad at liftoff. Fifty minutes later, twin sonic booms announced to our waiting friends and family that we had reentered Earth's atmosphere.

Our drag chute deployed and jettisoned, and we touched down at runway fifteen at Kennedy Space Center. We took off our pressure suits and, after completing our last few procedures, carefully disembarked from the shuttle. I took a last look around. I had spent ten years chasing space. And I had finally caught it.

The best part of coming home was seeing my family and friends and the immense joy and pride I felt while walking on terra firma again. It was a beautiful moment.

Walking on the beach that first morning after, looking at the horizon as the sun rose, knowing what was up and what was down—something that doesn't really apply in space—made me marvel at the majesty of God's creations and how fortunate I'd been to get to experience a little piece of it from a whole different point of view.

Going to space changes a person on so many different levels. I wouldn't have been able to accomplish any of what I accomplished in space without a strong team, and my mission really brought home the power of teamwork. People can accomplish amazing things when they work together.

I also learned to see all human beings as potential space travelers—no matter what language they speak, food they eat, or what they look like. We're all orbiting the sun on this small blue planet together. We can work together to make the world a better place, but first we have to be willing to accept and value one another.

From the vantage point of space, our planet looks like a little blue marble. That vantage point changes you. Astronauts call this the orbital shift—the moment when you begin to think differently about yourself and the world. My orbital shift happened after breaking bread with my international crewmates in space. It showed me how close we are as countries, as races, as species. I marveled how on Earth we have all these distances and separations and geographical boundaries, and how they vanish entirely in the weightless interior of the space station.

I'd always been a low-key guy, my calm born from the strength of my upbringing and the bedrock of my faith. In those moments of worry, I always found solace walking in the fields of Serenity Farm or in the simple wisdom of 2 Timothy 1:7. "For the Spirit God gave us does not make us timid, but gives us power, love, and self-discipline." Still, when I got back from space, I realized that so many of the things that I thought were a big deal were no longer so important. I'd been in space! Nothing could ever take that from me.

Being earthbound again didn't mean that I stayed in one place. In April 2008, nearly two months after my return from space, I went to back to PRH to talk to the kids about my trip and to return the quilt they'd made me. It had traveled nearly 5.3 million miles and circled Earth 203 times. In June, I joined the SST-122 crew on a journey to Germany to celebrate our successful installation of the Columbus Laboratory and Léopold Eyharts's historic accomplishment as the first European astronaut to live on the space station for an extended stay. Then I traveled to Israel to play in a Pro-Am tennis tournament and to honor the memory of the first Israeli astronaut, Ilan Ramon, who had died in the *Columbia* disaster.

Because of my experience with the Educator Astronaut Program, I was also called on to speak to groups of children while traveling in Israel. I shared my stories of space travel with children who lived in cities that had been repeatedly hit by rocket fire in the ongoing war between the Israelis and the Palestinians.

"No matter what happens in our lives, we have to keep moving forward," I told them. "We have to keep doing our best, no matter what the circumstances. It is about your heart, dedication, and spirit."

Wherever I went, I told my young audiences that few people I knew possessed as much of those qualities as Ilan, Israel's fallen astronaut.

When I returned to Houston, it was time to start training for a new role—that of a Cape Crusader.

CHAPTER 13
CAPE CRUSADER

Back in Houston in August 2008, I took up training as a Cape Crusader. That sounds like Batman's job in Gotham City, but Cape Crusaders actually play a vital role on every space mission. Behind every shuttle crew, there is a team of five to eight astronauts who serve as the crew's contact between JSC in Houston and NASA-Kennedy Space Center (KSC) on the Florida coast. Cape Crusaders are the eyes and ears to the shuttle vehicle. Other than being on the flight crew itself, it's the best astronaut job to have.

A Cape Crusader also helps get astronauts into their

seats on the shuttle and conducts communication checks with Mission Control Command (MCC). But helping out our fellow astronauts and MCC wasn't our only role. In today's dangerous world, the Kennedy Space Center has a highly trained SWAT team in place to protect the center and its astronauts from any troublemakers. Crusaders are given firearms training to help the SWAT team in the event of a terrorist attack.

I was immersed in my Crusader training when Kent Rominger, the chief of the astronaut office at the time, called me into his office and told me that in November, I would be going into space again. I'd been assigned to shuttle mission STS-129 to bring spare parts and other essential replacement components to the space station. These components were to be "staged," or attached, to the outside of the ISS using the robotic arm.

My fellow Cape Crusader Barry "Butch" Wilmore was going to pilot the mission, his first. We'd be joining commander Charlie "Scorch" Hobaugh and mission specialists Randy Bresnik, Mike Foreman, and Bobby Satcher. Randy and Bobby would both be going on spacewalks, while Butch and I flew the robotic arms.

I was excited and shocked to be named to the mission since it had not been that long since I had flown. But I certainly wasn't going to turn down a chance to go back to space!

I have been asked if being part of the astronaut corps affected my sense of time. It certainly did in the sense that I knew I had only so many weeks to train to be perfect. If you are not perfect, seriously perfect, you can kill yourself, someone else, or the entire team. Having flown before in no way diminished my sense of how high the stakes were during the months of training for my second mission.

In the midst of our training, Barack Obama won his first term as president. I was fortunate enough to be able to attend his inauguration in January 2009. I watched with a tremendous sense of pride as a black man took the oath of office for our nation's highest job.

I remember hearing world-class musicians Anthony McGill, Itzhak Perlman, Yo-Yo Ma, and Gabriela Montero perform composer John Williams's "Air and Simple Gifts." Few things could match the thrill of such an extraordinary and historic occasion—except maybe going back to space.

The training for my next mission followed a typical routine. Over the next several months, it was full of exercises and simulations. The repetition could get tedious, but just as before, our absolute attention to every detail was critical.

But in the midst of it, a welcome break came my way. A few years after I got Jake, a second dog that looked almost exactly like him showed up on my lawn. I'd seen him wandering around my neighborhood before. He had no collar, he was nearly blind, and as I soon learned, he had heartworms. I knew he must have had a home nearby, but his owners clearly didn't care about him, so I named him Scout and took him in as my own.

Now I had two nearly identical Rhodesian Ridgeback mixes—both of whom had come to me by accident. Scout was relatively mild-mannered, a nice contrast to Jake's considerably more excitable personality. Jake protected me like a grizzly bear defending her cub. He sometimes tried to bite people who came too close.

My good friend and fellow astronaut Suni Williams had a Jack Russell terrier named Gorby (after former Soviet leader Mikhail Gorbachev), who was also having discipline problems. He had the unfortunate habit of chasing after dogs bigger than him. He hadn't gotten hurt yet—but Suni was sure it was only a matter of time.

The NASA public relations department caught wind of our dog problems and decided to turn them into publicity. They reached out to Cesar Millan, star of National Geographic's *Dog Whisperer*, and on a sunny day in May, Cesar drove down to Houston in his custom-built RV to help us out. The episode of his TV show was titled "Cesar, We Have a Problem."

"Astronauts Suni Williams and Leland Melvin have been flawless in space but are experiencing technical difficulties with their dogs here on Planet Earth," the show's narrator said. "Cesar likes to tackle the toughest problem first, so he begins with Leland and Jake."

When Jake started to act up, Cesar noted a change in my demeanor. He told viewers, "That joyful, calm, passionate astronaut went out the window." The minute Cesar came into the house, Jake started to growl and show his teeth. I thought Jake might actually kill the poor guy. Then I realized Jake was confusing Cesar with the El Lago garbage men who used to taunt him through the window when they picked up the trash cans near the back door.

I had Jake on a leash and he was lurching after the TV host. Cesar's advice was to stay as calm as I could and let go of the leash. Jake needed to know that Cesar wasn't going to hurt me. If I was relaxed, Jake would settle down. And Cesar was right. Soon Jake was sitting calmly at my feet.

Cesar explained that anytime I had Jake on a leash and was feeling tension, Jake was picking up on that.

"When you need to correct him, correct him very quickly, and then take the tension out of the leash," Cesar explained.

That was great advice, not just with Jake, but also with my robotics training. Making sure my hands weren't tense when I was holding on to the controls, trying to be as loose and free as possible, made the robotics movements both smoother and more accurate.

It was a great metaphor for life, too. Whatever you put into something is what you get out of it. Putting tension or drama into a task just fills it with tension and drama.

Cesar was equally helpful with Suni and Gorby.

I was already a minor celebrity—at least to people who followed the space program—but being on the show brought me a slightly higher level of fame. Suddenly, I had to get used to being recognized outside of Houston.

In September, I was fortunate enough to get to be a part of another inspiring collaboration. In 2005, in the aftermath of the devastation of Hurricane Katrina, I started to write poetry to express my heartbreak over the devastation in New Orleans. I never thought that I would share it with anyone. The words were just for my own sense of healing, but at a celebration of the fortieth anniversary of spaceflight at the Stephen F. Udvar-Hazy Space Center, one of the Smithsonian's National Air and Space Museums, I had to the chance to meet Grammy Award–winning singer-songwriter and record producer Pharrell Williams. Our discussion sparked his imagination, and in September I flew to Miami to read him my poem, "Exploration." It begins:

The journey of a city made in haste
Many people frown about the waste
Cluttered minds and empty souls

Wonder how we will one day behold
The world without treasures found today
In the atmosphere far away
Floating around the heavens we see
Advancing the future with harmony
Seen in galaxies miles away
Solutions to the crisis in the world today

Pharrell was inspired to write music to go along with my lyrics. The finished product arrived in the mail a week later, and I promised him that I would play our song when I got back up in space.

LIFTOFF

We launched at 14:28 (2:28 p.m.) EDT on Monday, November 16, 2009, on a mission to build, resupply, and do research on the International Space Station. We shimmied in our seats as the engines came to life and the rockets fired. And like that, I was off to space—again.

We had a variety of tasks on our to-do list, most of them focusing on staging spare components outside the space station. When you're in space and something breaks, you can't exactly run down to the corner hardware store. We carried everything from spare nitrogen tanks to battery chargers to parts for the robotic arms, and materials to help with experiments done on board the station. Many of these parts would be attached to the outside of the space station, ready for when the astronauts on board might need them.

A few hours after we got to space, we were all working hard, following many of the same procedures as my first space flight. A couple of the rookies were feeling sick and moving slowly, but I felt fine, at first. But about six hours in, I began to make strange sounds, sort of like a turkey gobbling. Here's the thing about being in microgravity—the air in your stomach doesn't separate from the food the way it does on Earth. On Earth we can sense when we're going to burp and when we're about to throw up. That's not always true in space.

Before I knew it, I was barfing my brains out. I grabbed for a barf bag, but I didn't have quite enough time. Green fluid came out of my mouth and bounced up against the rim of my University of Richmond hat before bouncing down on my eyebrows and mixing into my mustache. Welcome to being sick in space!

After I cleaned myself up, I felt fine. I went back to work—checking the outside of the orbiter for any damage, making sure the robotic arm was working, and preparing for the upcoming spacewalks.

We docked with the International Space Station on day three and met with the station crew. Commander Frank De Winne welcomed us, along with Jeffrey Williams, Robert

Thirsk, Nicole Stott, and cosmonauts Roman Romanenko and Maxim Suraev.

We didn't waste any time getting to work. The same day we docked, Randy and I used the shuttle's robotic arm to lift important materials out of the payload bay. We handed it over to the station's robotic arm, which was operated by Butch and Jeffrey. They permanently installed the carrier to the outside of the station. The following day, Bobby and Mike performed our first spacewalk and completed their tasks—attaching the spare parts to the space station—without a hitch. That night, however, a false depressurization alarm sounded and woke us, but flight control teams on the ground determined there was no danger to the station or crew. It was the first of three alarms that would sound during our mission, all of which proved false.

That said, had the alarms signaled real emergencies, we would have been prepared. Everything about NASA's training drives home the point that space is an incredibly dangerous place. If you do something wrong out there, it's game over. The biggest emergency is depressurization. A sudden drop in air pressure can be deadly. Everything we do in space revolves around keeping the oxygen sealed in. If we can't breathe, we're toast. And for all its sophistication, the ISS really is just a technologically advanced tin can. If something hits the space station hard enough, it's going to cause a breach. And if the air gets out, everyone inside will die. If that first alarm had been real, emergency protocol would have been for us to go straight to our vehicle and to close the hatches. We would have had only minutes to get in, make sure it was safe, and head home.

Another emergency we train for relentlessly is fire. If a fire alarm were to go off, our computer screens would display the module where fire was suspected. Then we would go to the location to see if we could identify smoke or flames. There's never been a fire on the space station, but we've all been trained to handle one just in case. You can't exactly call the fire department when you're 240 miles above Earth. Fire extinguishers are always at the ready should we need one.

Solar flares present another kind of danger. These sudden flashes of light near the sun's surface can send dangerous high-energy particles into space. These flares rarely breach Earth's atmosphere, but the radiation in them can be dangerous to astronauts on the space station. If there's a solar flare, all the astronauts float up into the doghouse, a space at the top of the ISS surrounded with water bags, until Houston gives us the all clear. The water absorbs the radiation and keeps it from traveling into our bodies.

As astronauts, we're trained to not be alarmed by things. We're trained to ask, "How will I fix this?" first.

Everything we do to prepare for our trips is done to make us self-sufficient. No one can help you out in space. You have to be able to handle whatever is sent your way.

On our third spacewalk, EVA 3, for instance, Butch Wilmore and I were supporting Bobby and Randy with the robotic arm. We were moving an oxygen tank from ELC-2 that needed to be installed outside an airlock. Butch and I got a little behind. While we were moving the arm in for the grapple, we had not configured the business end of it, the End Effector (EE). The EE had a canister at the end of the arm and was used to attach the arm to payloads. It contained three wires that wrapped around the target grapple pin on the oxygen tank that allowed us to connect the tank to the arm.

Butch was flying the arm, and I was supporting him. It looked like we weren't ready to capture the tank, because the EE wires were not properly configured, but I told Butch to keep moving the arm, that it was going to be okay. I had successfully worked the arm during my first mission and had confidence that we would be successful again.

That was a great moment between the two of us. We saved time by capturing the tank without having to stop and reset everything.

EVA 2 had been eventful, too, but for a different reason. When Bobby and I worked together to move ELC-2 out of the shuttle payload bay and hand it off to the space station's robotic arm, we helped resolve a long-standing historical injustice. Forty-three years after racism forced Ed Dwight, the first African-American astronaut candidate, from the program, Bobby and I became the first African-American men to fly together on an EVA shuttle mission. He was outside on the arm while I flew it using the controls in the ISS.

For such a historic moment, it was pretty subdued. But looking down at our planet then, I know that both Bobby and I were aware of the significance. Seeing the world without geographic boundaries really puts things in perspective. It makes you wonder why there is so much division, hatred, and malice; it made me want to raise the bar and ensure that all people, everywhere, were empowered to chase their dreams and live the lives they aspired to.

We shared these sentiments the next day from space on the *Tom Joyner Morning Show*, the popular syndicated radio program. Bobby and I fielded questions from the host while reaching out to young listeners. We talked about some of the experiments we were conducting in conjunction with researchers from Texas Southern University and Delaware State University, two historically black colleges. The first studied how microbes grow under weightless conditions. The second involved developing optical instruments for space operations. We also offered a message especially for younger listeners. "They can achieve anything they put their minds to if they believe in themselves and stay determined," I told Tom. "Anybody can do this job. You just have to be focused and determined and just make it happen."

Every crew has its own chemistry, and we started to get ours very early, before our rendezvous with the ISS. Scorch told a kind of stupid joke about two friends going water-skiing on a boat called the *FishBro*. They were first-time skiers and didn't know what they were doing. When the one guy asked the other if he was ready, his friend replied, "Make it happen, Captain." The boat accelerated, but the slack in the rope launched the rookie skier into the air. The joke was kind of stupid, but from that point on, "Make it happen, Captain" became our catchphrase. For example, while operating the arm, I asked Bobby if he was ready to move to a specific location. He answered, "Make it happen, Captain."

Our spacewalks successfully completed, it was time to head home. We had gone to space with six crew members but we flew home with seven. Flight engineer Nicole Stott had been in space for ninety-one days and we were her ride home.

We actually were able to complete several tasks ahead of schedule, which left us a little time to just enjoy our trip to space. As with other missions, we all brought carefully selected mementos to space. Randy's items included a scarf worn by the famous American aviation pioneer Amelia Earhart. My own artifacts included a photograph by artist Elaine Duigenan and a T-shirt from Pharrell Williams's BBC ICECREAM clothing line. Bobby recorded me floating in microgravity while playing "Exploration," the song Pharrell and I had written together.

My future plans continued to take shape in my mind as we completed our mission. The rhythms of "Exploration" lingered like a refrain in my head:

Floating around the heavens we see

Advancing the future with harmony.

Being more involved in the arts changed my own notion of what I wanted to do next. My interest in relying on a STEM foundation to educate and inspire people had expanded to one that made room for arts, or STEAM. I planned to do a lot more with STEAM after I returned to Earth.

CHAPTER 14

EDUCATOR ASTRONAUT

The *Atlantis* landed at the Kennedy Space Center the day after Thanksgiving, November 27, 2009. The cooks at crew quarters outdid themselves preparing a Thanksgiving feast for us to share with our families.

And I had so much to be thankful for. My sister, my good friend Mary Gordon, and my parents had all traveled to Florida to see me come home safely. We had successfully installed ELC-1 and ELC-2 on the space station, and we brought Nicole back to her family. I slept really well that night. Unlike my first night back from STS-122, I didn't wake up wondering if I was still in space.

In the morning, we boarded a jet back to Ellington Field, near the JSC in Texas, and received a heroes' welcome. Then it was time to settle back into regular life—if being an astronaut can ever be called "regular."

The whole crew got together a month later at a Houston Texans football game. I had caught a few balls in space wearing the jersey of the team's leading receiver, Andre Johnson, and had the whole crew sign it. At the game, I returned it to Andre, but that wasn't the highlight of the day. That came when we stood next to former president George H. W. Bush on the sidelines singing "The Star-Spangled Banner."

I began 2010 at NASA headquarters in Washington, DC. The Summer of Innovation program was my chance to inspire the next generation of space explorers. Too many kids "slump" over the summer, forgetting what they learned over the course of the school year. This program was all about making scientific discovery and space exploration exciting. We worked hard to help kids learn while they were having fun with STEM-related games and experiments.

Soon I decided to make my role in NASA's education program more formal. I wanted to be involved in more than the summer program, so I applied to be NASA's associate administrator of education. That meant I would be working with NASA, Congress, and schools around the country to make sure that kids got the kind of education they needed to contribute to the space program.

I also started a nontraditional partnership between NASA Education and the rapper and actor Yasiin Bey, who also goes by the stage name Mos Def. Mos Def used his music to teach kids about the science of sound waves and to get them excited about the parallels between music, science, and math. Mos was filmed teaching the science of sound waves, and we created holographic images of the two of us talking about the parallels between music and science to show to kids around the country.

Working with NASA Education and later the White House Committee on STEM Education gave me the opportunity to bring together thinkers and artists. Our goal was to inspire young people to engage the world and explore. We even partnered with LEGO to create these really cool robotics kits. The LEGO sets—two small LEGO shuttles—were flown to the International Space Station in February 2011. Astronauts in orbit and children and student groups across the country assembled the kits at the same time to demonstrate how objects behave differently in the zero gravity of space compared to gravity on Earth.

I also had the chance to travel all over the world. Perhaps the most exciting trip was to Africa. I met with members of the new South African National Space Agency and asked them to join our International Space Education Board. In a recent study, South Africa came in almost dead last in math and science education—Egypt and Paraguay were the only countries that ranked lower. Kids in South Africa weren't getting the chance to learn about why space exploration is so important. And most of them have no idea that they can be a part of it. I try to make it my responsibility to show children from all over the world how they can become space professionals.

Back in the United States, singer, songwriter, actor, and record producer will.i.am, another friend Lars Perkins, and I came up with a program we called Stimulating Youth in STEM (SYSTEM). Our goal is to motivate young people to get involved in science, math, and the arts.

When the Mars rover *Curiosity* was launched at Cape Canaveral on November 26, 2011, the three of us were on hand to watch. will.i.am was so inspired by the launch he assembled a children's choir and composed a song with them called "Reach for the Stars." When *Curiosity* landed on Mars, flight controllers beamed the song to the rover, and the rover beamed it back to Earth again. It had completed a journey of more than 700 million miles from Earth to Mars and back again. It was the first interplanetary song ever—and the NASA jet propulsion laboratory engineer, Bobak Ferdowsi, became the first interplanetary DJ when he started playing the song by flipping a switch.

* * *

During one of my trips to promote reading and encourage underserved students to consider careers in science—this was toward the end of 2012—my neighbor called to let me know that my dog Scout wasn't doing well. She was watching him while he was being treated for lymphoma, but the treatment wasn't working. I flew home and rushed him to the hospital. Sadly, that night I had to put my dog to sleep. Scout had been a kind, loving dog, and I miss him still today.

In the beginning of 2013, I was part of a group of NASA engineers and astronauts in President Obama's second inauguration parade. As we passed the presidential viewing area, I saluted him and he saluted me back. Seeing him take the oath of office for the second time filled me with pride and reminded me that nothing is impossible. Nothing!

All the while, I continued to participate in STEAM events, rubbing elbows with celebrities like will.i.am and Mos Def, and even testifying about STEM education before Congress.

It was while I was in DC that I realized that Jake, my running partner of 15 years, was in serious trouble. The same dog that had raced up mountains with me could barely walk up the stairs. I could tell by the way he looked at me that his mind and body were worn out. I talked to the vet and decided that it would be kinder to put Jake to sleep than to make him continue to fight the pain. We spent a last day together at the arboretum listening to the sounds of the city. The next morning I took him to the vet and gave him the peaceful transition he deserved.

Soon afterward, I began to pack up my house in DC. Losing Jake and spending time with my aging parents had confirmed an idea that had been growing in my mind for some time. It was time to go back to Lynchburg. It was time to go home.

"I am sorry to inform the NASA family that my good friend and our associate administrator for education, Leland Melvin, has decided to retire next month after more than 24 years of NASA service," Charlie Bolden wrote in a January 2014 memo to my colleagues.

I had spent twenty-four years at NASA. I had been a research scientist at Langley and a doctoral student at the University of Maryland. I helped lead a team to create life-saving optical fiber sensors. I was an astronaut and an educator. My time with the space agency had been an incredible journey, and I would always have my NASA family in my heart.

I returned home on February 16 and had a wonderful conversation with my dad. He was eighty-three years old, and his health had been in decline for a number of years. Our roles had all but completely reversed. Now I was the one taking care of him. The very next day he collapsed and we rushed him to the hospital, but they were unable to save him.

Friends and family, including my mother, gathered at the hospital as soon as they heard the news. Our sadness quickly became a celebration of the wonderful life he had lived. We prayed and sang. Emotions turned to joy and gratitude for the time we had with him. I had moved home to be with him, and I would miss having my guide and mentor. Even today, even still, and probably forever more, I miss my dad.

In one way or another, my father taught me everything I know. He had introduced me to the principles of engineering when he converted that dilapidated bread truck to a family camper. He had encouraged me to read about places I could hardly fathom, to study maps to envision places I had never been. Just as the view from space illuminates connections on Earth that we can't see at ground level, my perspective as an adult helped me see the links between my father's teaching and NASA's mission. In the same way that my father had educated and inspired me, I wanted more than ever to continue my work educating and (hopefully) inspiring kids, parents, and teachers about space exploration. I knew that wherever my own future led me, I would continue to spread the word about possibilities and connections, lighting the path for journeys humanity has yet to take.

CHAPTER 15
THE NEXT MISSION

L ife after NASA brought many new opportunities. One included hosting a television show called *Child Genius* in which brilliant young people competed for a $100,000 college scholarship. Kids from across the country applied to be a part of the show. Producers chose contestants based on their grades, their IQ scores, and their competitive spirits. The first season took place over the course of eight weeks, testing the nation's brightest young minds on their knowledge of just about everything.

I had to study the questions and learn to pronounce crazy words like floccinaucinihilipilification (the act of judging something as useless). The questions could be crazy, too. For instance: Take the number of pairs of ribs the average human being has and multiply by each of the two numbers representing Grover Cleveland's presidencies. That's 12 multiplied by 22 multiplied by 24 for an answer of 6336.

I wasn't able to interact with the contestants off camera—the producers worried that might look like favoritism—but I was impressed by all of them. The competitors included Tanishq, a ten-year-old college freshman, and Katherine, a thirteen-year-old from California with an IQ of 140. Eight-year-old Madison stood up against kids four years older and held her own in the first two rounds of competition, but it was spelling whiz Vanya from Kansas who won it all the first season and went home with the trophy and a $100,000 college scholarship.

I was also impressed by the way the kids cheered for and supported one another both on and off camera, giving each other high fives when they did well and hugs when they didn't.

I loved the idea of a show that celebrated brainpower instead of crazy behavior, but unfortunately we were canceled after two seasons. Still, hosting a TV show was something I never expected to do.

Another unexpected opportunity came my way when I was asked to join the television show *BattleBots*—in which competitors had to design and operate robots decked out with flippers, powerful hammers, and other weapons. I got to judge the 2015 and 2016 seasons. The robots went head-to-head in an arena, and I was one of three judges who got to vote for the winner.

I didn't think judging a robotics contest would be dangerous. The box, or robot arena, was made of thick, bulletproof glass, after all. But in the second match of the day, a robot named Icewave had a blade weapon that spun at 300 miles per hour. It chipped a piece of metal off another bot. That piece of metal shot across the arena like a bullet and carved out a heavy chunk of glass right in front of our faces. Suddenly being in outer space felt safe!

BattleBots is the ultimate demonstration of the hands-on STEAM learning I had been advocating for years. It was exactly the kind of learning and experience the next generation will need to travel to Mars—and beyond.

And I do believe that someday humans will travel to Mars, but now more than ever I'm concerned with life on this planet.

In 1968, *Apollo 8* became the first manned spacecraft to enter lunar orbit. The photograph taken of Earth rising above the moon's crater-marked surface changed the way humans thought about our planet. That photo, known as "Earthrise," is often credited with starting the environmental movement.

It is, in part, why I teamed up with a group of international astronauts to make sure that Earth will still be here for generations to come. Our group, known as Constellation, is working together toward the "sustainable development" goals announced by the United Nations in 2015. These important goals include putting an end to poverty and hunger, making sure that everyone has access to clean water and quality education, combating climate change, and protecting life in the water and on land.

By banding together, we can do more than any one of us can do alone.

NASA'S NEXT MISSION

Just because I left the space agency doesn't mean I am any less interested in our future in space. I continue to follow NASA's news closely. New discoveries and technological advances are being made all the time.

In 2015 alone, NASA discovered flowing water on Mars and evidence of ice on one of Jupiter's moons. They were also able to map Pluto—a tiny nonplanetary object more than three billion miles away—using the space probe *New Horizons*.

Before leaving office, President Obama set clear goals for America's next chapter in space: "Sending humans to Mars by the 2030s and returning them safely to Earth, with the ultimate ambition to one day remain there for an extended time."

Living on Mars will present some special challenges. The astronauts might be on another planet, but most of their time will be spent isolated in a small spacecraft or in a Martian habitat. Imagine living inside of your house with just a few other people for three years without ever going outside or even being able to open a window! And if you want to go outside, first you have to put on a bulky space suit that functions as its own mini space station. On top of that, because of the challenges of having enough water in space, astronauts might have to wear the same pair of underwear for months at a time!

President Obama was right when he said that "getting [to Mars] will take a giant leap. But the first, small steps happen when our students—the Mars generation—walk into their classrooms each day. Scientific discovery doesn't happen with the flip of a switch; it takes years of testing, patience, and a national commitment to education."

Today NASA is developing the most advanced rocket and spacecraft ever designed to send humans farther into the solar system than ever before, including to an asteroid and to Mars. There is already a fleet of robotic explorers on and around the Red Planet.

At the same time, multiple NASA missions are studying

our sun and the solar system, searching for answers to questions humans have asked since the beginning of time.

And national agencies like NASA aren't the only ones taking on the challenge of space exploration. Private companies started by space entrepreneurs like Richard Branson and Elon Musk are developing vehicles to send astronauts, private citizens, and cargo into space.

Not long ago I sat with my mother on the porch of her nursing home, looking up at the moon.

"Mom, we should go there because you won't need your wheelchair," I said.

She smiled. "Okay."

"Three days there, three days back, and one to bounce on the surface. A week's vacation and we'll be home again."

She laughed and turned to me. "Let's go!"

Humans have a deep desire to explore uncharted territory. I believe that desire will take us back to the moon and then on to the Red Planet. One day there will be human footsteps on Mars. Will they be yours?

When Leland wanted to buy a new skateboard, his father challenged him to build one. He soon learned how different aspects of design—the length and shape of the board or the size of the wheels—could change how fast the skateboard would go. Follow the directions on the following pages to construct your own rocket-propelled vehicle. You can experiment with ways to increase the distance your racer travels or its speed by modifying your design—just like Leland experimented with ways to make his skateboard go faster!

If you build your racer with friends, you can hold drag races for speed or compete for distance. In this activity, you will investigate basic forces that affect motion—*position*, *velocity*, and *acceleration*. All of these are related to Isaac Newton's laws of motion, which govern our world and provide the foundation for rocket science.

The three laws of motion deal with position, velocity, and acceleration:

Position is an explanation of where something is, based on a certain origin (or starting place).

Velocity is the speed and direction something is moving.

Acceleration is how velocity changes with time.

You can find out more about Newton's three laws of motion in the *Adventures in Rocket Science* activity guide referenced at the end of this experiment or by searching educational resources available at NASA.gov.

191

NOTES AS YOU BEGIN

⚠️ Safety first! Always wear properly fitting goggles for experiments. And always make sure to have an adult supervising your work.

❏ If you don't have a compass, you can trace circular objects to make the wheels or use the wheel and hubcap patterns provided.

❏ Styrofoam cup bottoms can also be used as wheels. Putting hubcaps on both sides of the wheels may improve performance.

❏ Be sure to conduct your experiment on a stable, smooth surface such as a tile floor or carpeted floors with a short nap.

❏ Once you create and race your first vehicle, think about how to modify or improve your design and try it again!

❏ Be sure to measure how far your racer travels with each launch and track your data!

PROCEDURE

For this experiment, the first step is to build your rocket racer. Once you construct and test your initial vehicle you can modify the design to improve distance or speed and compare results.

1. Lay out the patterns for your vehicle parts on a Styrofoam tray. You need 1 car body, 4 wheels, and 4 hubcaps. Use

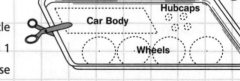

a compass to draw the wheels or trace the circles from other items such as a tin can or paper cup. (You can also trace the wheel and hubcap patterns provided.)

192

Cut out the vehicle parts.

2. Blow up the balloon and then let the air out. Tape the balloon to the short end of a flexible straw and then tape the straw to the vehicle body (the long rectangle). This is the top of your vehicle. Make sure you leave enough of the straw hanging over the end of the vehicle body so you can blow up the balloon and then pinch the straw between your fingers.

3. Add wheels and hubcaps to your vehicle body by using the pins. Push the pins through the hubcaps into the wheels and then into the edges of the Styrofoam rectangle.

4. Blow up the balloon through the straw. Squeeze the end of the straw to hold the air in until you are ready to race. Place the racer on the floor and let it go!

QUESTIONS TO INVESTIGATE

In this experiment, you were introduced to the laws of motion by launching your air-propelled vehicle across a smooth surface. The force of the expelled air changes the *position* of your vehicle by propelling it across the floor. You observed its *velocity* as it moved and noticed a change in *acceleration* due to a decrease of air in the balloon over time. These are the basic concepts that provide the foundation for rocket science.

The study of motion is fundamental to understanding the dynamic properties of an object and how they are affected by factors such as altitude and weight, air temperature, or density. From experiments like this one, you can also see how concepts such as measurement and rate of change are important in designing vehicles and rockets.

Now that you have built your first racer and recorded your results, consider other variables that might affect the outcome. What other factors might affect the speed or distance your vehicle can travel? Put another way: What forces could be slowing down your rocket racer?

Formulate new questions as you think about modifying your design to test for variables. Some suggested questions may be:

▶ *What resistance did your racer encounter?*

  (Air resistance, obstacles on the racing surface?)

▶ *Would a different type of material, such as cardboard, improve performance?*

▶ *How can I modify the design to improve the racer's speed?*

▶ *How can I modify the design to improve the racer's distance?*

▶ *What happens if I use a bigger balloon, larger wheels, or a bigger straw?*

As you change the design of your racer to investigate the effect of an individual variable, keep track of your changes and results so you can compare and analyze them. Use the graph paper to draw out the dimensions and shapes before you trace and cut your pattern. Think about how your racer will look from the side, the front, and the top.

IDEAS FOR EXTRA FUN!

Hold rocket racer races! Have a group of friends design and build individual racers and compete. To make sure each racer starts with the same amount of air:

1. Make sure everyone uses the same-size balloon.

2. Tie a loop of string around an inflated balloon attached to one of the racers.

3. Create a loop of string of the same size for each racer, or use one loop and launch the racers individually.

4. Inflate each balloon inside the string loop each time you test the racers. This will help ensure the balloon inflates the same amount each time.

WHEEL PATTERNS

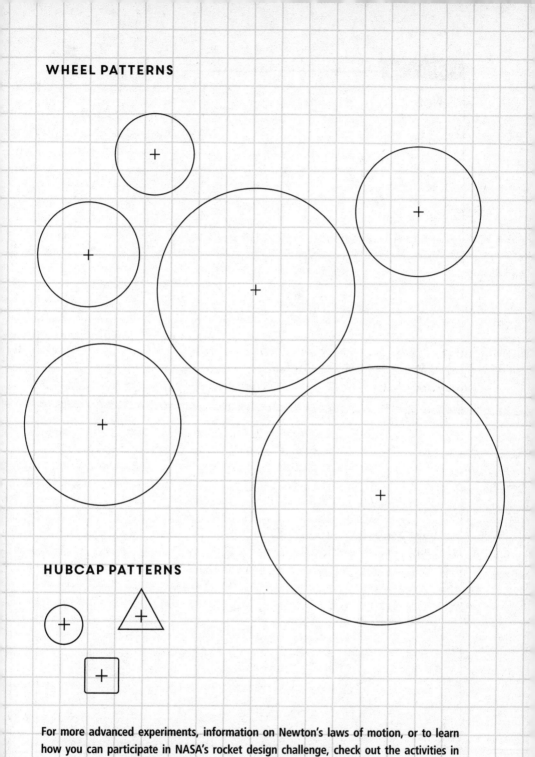

HUBCAP PATTERNS

For more advanced experiments, information on Newton's laws of motion, or to learn how you can participate in NASA's rocket design challenge, check out the activities in www.nasa.gov/pdf/265386main_Adventures_In_Rocket_Science.pdf.

Notes:

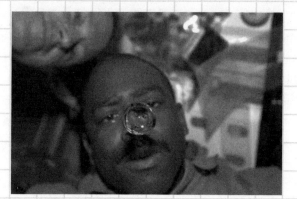

The image of Leland eating candies floating inside a water bubble was taken on board the International Space Station during STS-122. (You can also check out the video at www.youtube.com/watch?v=edPZYCRPgu0.) Astronauts use water to capture floating food particles and "drink" them down while living in zero-gravity environments.

Astronauts conduct experiments in space to determine how certain elements and chemical components will respond to a new environment. While you won't conduct your experiment in space (just yet!), you can learn a lot right here on Earth, in your own kitchen.

Check out the video from the space station. Leland ate his M&M's before we were able to observe if the water had any effect on the candy coating. In this activity, you will answer the basic question, *What happens to candy coating in water?* As you follow the procedure and conduct the experiment, be sure to record your observations. After you gather the results, you can alter the design and create your own experiment!

MATERIALS YOU WILL NEED

- Sweets/chocolates with a colored candy coating (like M&M's, Reese's Pieces, or Skittles)
- White plastic or foam plates • Room-temperature water • Measuring cup • Crayons or colored pencils • Container for discarded water • Paper towels • Timer or watch • Paper

⚠️ Safety first! Always wear properly fitting goggles for experiments. And always make sure to have an adult supervising your work.

❏ Be sure to conduct your experiment on a stable surface in a room where spills can be easily cleaned up.

❏ For best results, use plates with the flattest bottoms possible. Any size plate will work, but smaller plates require less water.

❏ A drawing can be an effective record of observation. Use the crayons and colored pencils to draw and record your results.

❏ Use the container to discard liquid from the plates after each experiment is complete. Dispose of the discarded water appropriately.

❏ You can dry the plates with paper towels so that the plates can be used more than once.

OBSERVE

For this experiment, the first step is observation. Observe your candy and note any basic characteristics such as:

▶ Size, shape, color, and texture

▶ Does it have different colored layers on the inside?

▶ Does it have additional ingredients (nuts, etc.)?

You may need to cut or break open a few pieces of candy to find out all of the characteristics, but be careful! You may be tempted to bite them in two—but resist the urge! It is never recommended to eat or drink items from your experiment!

PROCEDURE

1. Use one plate for one candy. Measure and pour enough room-temperature water into the plate so that the water is deep enough to completely cover the candy.

2. Once the water has settled, place one candy in the center of the plate. Be careful to keep the water and candy as still as possible so you can observe what happens without agitating the water.

198

3. Observe for about one minute without disturbing the plate.

4. Record your results in writing or with a drawing.

5. To repeat with a different-colored candy, discard your water in the container, dry the plate, and begin again. For comparable results with different-colored candies, use the same amount of water each time.

QUESTIONS TO INVESTIGATE

In this experiment, you saw what happened to candy coating when it was exposed to water. The coating dissolved. That's because candy coating is made up mostly of sugar and sugar dissolves in water. But why does sugar dissolve in water when other substances do not?

Some of the basic chemistry concepts you can investigate to answer that question include:

▶ *Molecules and charge. A water molecule has an area of positive charge and an area of negative charge.*

▶ *How molecules attract and interact based on their charge.*

▶ *How dissolving a substance depends on the interaction between molecules—in our case, how the water molecules interact with the molecules of sugar in the candy coating.*

What other questions would you ask based on your observations?

▶ *Did the dissolving sugar create a pattern in the water?*

▶ *Did the color float or sink?*

▶ *Did the inside chocolate or filling also dissolve? Why not?*

These are all good questions to investigate—and that is what chemistry is all about! Leland's love for science started with a chemistry set and a lot of questions, so keep investigating!

DESIGN YOUR OWN

Now that you have observed what happens when a candy is placed in a plate of room-temperature water, consider other variables and tweak the design of the experiment to test different variables.

In scientific inquiry, a *variable* is something that can affect the outcome of the experiment. Think about the different variables that may affect how the candy coating dissolves in water:

▶ *The color of the candy coating*

▶ *The number of candies on the plate*

▶ *The temperature of the water*

▶ *Adding sugar to your water solution*

Are there any other variables you can think of that you can test? What else could you change about the water you use to cover the candy?

Based on the variables above, formulate new questions and consider how you can alter the design of the basic experiment to test for each variable and answer your new question. Some suggested questions may be:

▶ *What happens if I make the water hotter?*

▶ *Does every color dissolve at the same rate?*

▶ *What happens if there are multiple candies on the same plate?*

▶ *What happens if I change the depth of the water?*

▶ *What happens if the water is sweet or salty?*

As you change the design of your experiment to investigate the effect of an individual variable, keep track of your change and results so you can compare and analyze them. Additional materials you may need as you alter the basic experiment to answer your new questions may be:

• Clear plastic containers (like small deli cups or drink cups)	• Quarter or other small circular object to trace circles	• Permanent marker
		• Measuring tape or ruler
		• Sugar or salt
• Hot tap water	• Plastic cups of different sizes to trace circles	• Teaspoon
• Cold water		

NOTES

Be careful when handling hot water.

If you want to see if one color dissolves faster than another, create boundary lines on your plate using a permanent marker to trace circles onto the plate (like a target) around a centered dot. Different-colored candies will be placed on the center dot of each plate.

Leland launched into space for the first time in February 2008 aboard the space shuttle *Atlantis*. His mission was made possible by decades of research and experimentation in aeronautics, rocket design, and fuel systems. NASA and other private, commercial companies are constantly improving the design of rockets and vehicles used for space travel, missions to the International Space Station, and maybe one day, the journey to Mars.

These experiments are an introduction in learning to design and build rockets. In the level-one activity, *Build a Paper Rocket*, you will construct a simple design to demonstrate how a rocket flies through the atmosphere. Basic concepts such as stability and control are introduced as you design and launch your rocket.

The size of the rocket as well as the size, number, and design of the fins can greatly affect stability and distance achieved. A rocket with no fins is much more difficult to control than a rocket with fins. The placement and size of the fins is critical to achieve adequate stability while not adding too much weight.

The level-two activity, *Water Bottle Rocket Assembly*, reinforces more advanced concepts associated with Newton's laws of motion such as the exertion of force to propel the rocket upward, showing the connection between force, propulsion, and acceleration.

The level-two activity includes instructions on how to test your rocket for stability and how to assemble a rocket launcher. It is recommended that you build the rocket launcher with adult assistance, as you will need to purchase items from a hardware or building supply store, as well as operate a drill. It is also recommended that you operate the rocket launcher with adult supervision and follow safety guidelines.

LEVEL ONE: BUILD A PAPER ROCKET

MATERIALS YOU WILL NEED

- Scrap bond paper
- Cellophane tape
- Scissors
- Sharpened fat pencil
- Milkshake straw

(slightly thinner than pencil)
- Eye protection
- Standard or metric ruler

- Masking tape or altitude trackers
- Pictures of the sun and planets

NOTES AS YOU BEGIN

⚠️ Safety first! Always wear properly fitting goggles for experiments. The rockets are projectiles, so wear eye protection. And always make sure to have an adult supervising your work.

❏ When launching rockets, it is important that others stand back. Use a countdown to help inform everyone as to liftoff!

❏ Collect a variety of decorative materials or decals before construction so you can customize the rockets.

❏ Be sure to conduct your experiment in a large area with enough space to allow for the rockets to fly.

❏ Once you create and launch your first paper rocket, think about how to modify or improve your design and try it again!

❏ Be sure to measure how far your rocket travels with each launch and track your data!

204

PROCEDURE

For this experiment, the first step is to build a paper rocket according to the diagram instructions provided. To test and fly the rocket, choose a large open space or hallway. Don't forget to use a measuring device (mark off measured sections with tape or lay out measuring sticks) so you can track the distance it flies.

Follow the arrows to build your rocket.

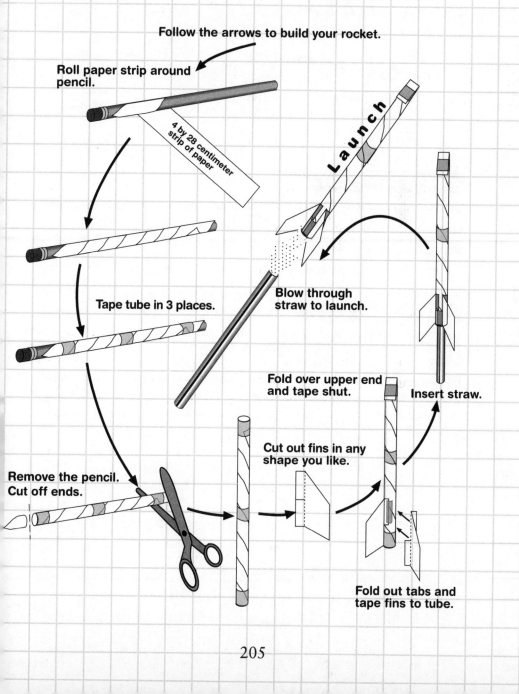

Roll paper strip around pencil.

4 by 28 centimeter strip of paper

Launch

Tape tube in 3 places.

Blow through straw to launch.

Fold over upper end and tape shut.

Insert straw.

Cut out fins in any shape you like.

Remove the pencil. Cut off ends.

Fold out tabs and tape fins to tube.

DESIGN YOUR OWN

Once you construct and test your initial paper rocket, you can modify the design to improve distance or stability and compare results. Think about the factors that might affect speed or the distance your rocket can travel. Though it is a simple paper rocket, how can you modify the design to conduct an experiment that tests for individual variables?

▶ *Can you change the shape or size of the fins?*

▶ *What happens if your rocket is larger (fatter than a pencil) or longer?*

▶ *What happens if you use a thicker or heavier paper to make your rocket?*

▶ *How many trips can your rocket sustain without damage?*

IDEAS FOR EXTRA FUN!

Use the planetary system chart provided on page 207 as a way to measure distance and think about interplanetary travel and what it might be like to launch from Earth into the solar system.

Research to discover how far each planet is from the sun and from Earth and create your system to scale according to the chart provided. Learn about the different planets' atmospheres and the difficulties humans may face when traveling through space.

For more detailed information on the science concepts demonstrated, as well as additional information on safety precautions and recording your results, you can reference the *Adventures in Rocket Science* activity guide or search educational resources available at NASA.gov.

PLANETARY SYSTEM CHART:

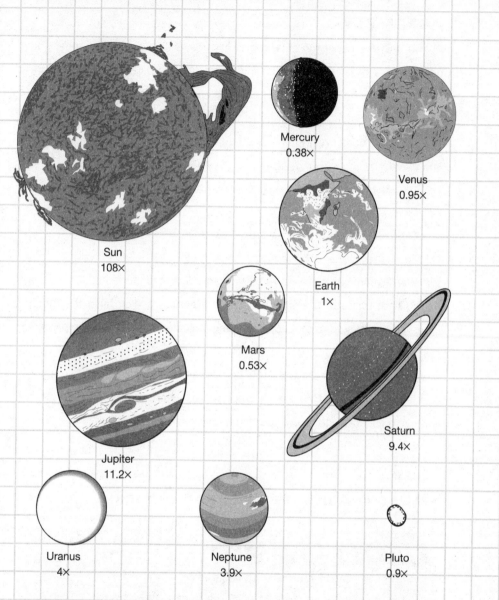

Sun
108×

Mercury
0.38×

Venus
0.95×

Earth
1×

Mars
0.53×

Jupiter
11.2×

Saturn
9.4×

Uranus
4×

Neptune
3.9×

Pluto
0.9×

Enlarge the planet images and color them to create your solar system, or sketch copies on separate paper. Place these pictures on the floor according to the Planetary System Chart. Make the planets to scale. Earth's diameter is given as one (1) and all the other bodies are given as multiples of one to show their size relative to Earth. (If Earth is one, then the sun is 108 times larger than Earth, and so on.)

LEVEL TWO: WATER BOTTLE ROCKET ASSEMBLY

As you built the paper rocket, you may have discovered how the number and design of fins affected stability and your ability to achieve distance. Now you are ready to expand on that exercise by building a water rocket that will fly by means of pressurized water. After your initial flight, you can think about how changes to fin design, rocket weight, or rocket length might improve the flight distance and speed.

The experiment has three stages:

Construction of the rocket

Construction of and performance of a stability test

Construction of a rocket launcher

We recommend that you work with an adult or under adult supervision during each phase of the experiment, but especially as you build the rocket launcher. You may want to read ahead, before you begin stage one, to prepare for each stage.

And remember, as always, safety first! Wear properly fitting safety goggles and launch your rockets in a large outdoor area where there is space to safely observe the launch and record your flight results.

STAGE ONE: BUILD THE WATER BOTTLE ROCKET

MATERIALS AND TOOLS

- 2-liter plastic soft drink bottles
- Low-temperature glue gun
- Poster board
- Tape (masking and/or duct)
- Scissors
- Safety glasses
- Decals
- Stickers
- Marker pens
- Small round ball or modeling clay

208

⚠ Safety first! Always wear properly fitting goggles for experiments, especially as you launch your rockets.

❑ Collect a variety of decorative materials or decals before construction so you can customize the rockets.

❑ Use tape or a low-temperature electric glue gun (available from craft stores) to attach the paper and decorations. High-temperature glue guns will melt the plastic bottles.

❑ Build your rockets on a surface where glue guns can be used safely, or put down a protective layer (such as flattened cardboard) over your workspace.

❑ When launching rockets, it is important that others stand back. Use a countdown to help inform everyone as to liftoff!

❑ Be sure to conduct your experiment in a large area with enough space to allow for the rockets to fly.

❑ Once you create and launch your first rocket, think about how to modify or improve your design and try it again!

❑ Be sure to measure how far your rocket travels with each launch and track your data!

PROCEDURE

For this experiment, the first step is to construct your rocket according to the diagram instructions provided. Test and launch the rockets using the rocket launcher in a large outdoor space.

1. Wrap poster board around the bottle to form the main tube of your rocket. Glue or tape it securely. The bottom of the plastic bottle will be the top of your rocket.

2. Design and cut out several fins of any size or shape and glue/tape them to the tube. The fins should align to the "bottom" of your rocket (which is the top opening of the plastic bottle).

3. Form a nose cone out of poster board and secure it with tape or glue.

4. Press a small round ball or modeling clay into the top of the nose cone.

5. Glue or tape the nose cone to the upper end of your rocket (the bottom of the

bottle) so that it may be easily removed. Performing the stage-two stability test will tell you if you need to add weight to your nose cone for stability.

6. Decorate your rocket.

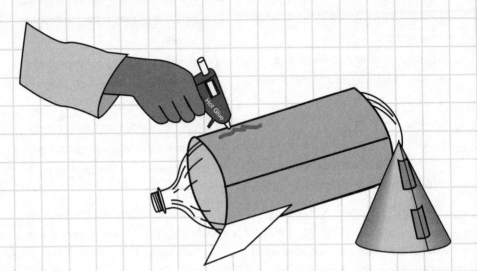

Once you have constructed your rocket, evaluate its quality of construction and design:

▸ *Observe how well fins align and how well they are spaced.*

▸ *Observe how smoothly the fins and nose cone attach to the bottle.*

▸ *Observe how straight the nose cone is at the top of the rocket.*

▸ *Observe how heavy your rocket is and how stable it seems to be as it sits on the table.*

Stability is an important factor in determining a rocket's ability to fly well. The next step in our experiment is to construct and perform the stability test.

STAGE TWO: PERFORM THE STRING-SWING STABILITY TEST

A rocket that flies straight through the air is said to be a stable rocket. A rocket that veers off course or tumbles wildly is said to be an unstable rocket. The difference between the flight of a stable rocket and an unstable rocket depends upon its design.

All rockets have two distinct centers. The first is the center of mass (CM). This is a point about which the rocket balances. If you could place a ruler edge under this point, the rocket would balance horizontally like a seesaw. What this means is that half of the mass of the rocket is on one side of the ruler edge, and half is on the other. The CM should be toward the rocket's nose.

The other center in a rocket is the center of pressure (CP). This is a point where half of the surface area of a rocket is on one side and half is on the other. The CP should be toward the rocket's tail for the rocket to fly straight, as the fins and tail have more surface area. (To learn more about the center of mass and center of pressure, consult the *Adventures in Rocket Science* PDF after your experiment is complete!)

MATERIALS AND TOOLS

- A spool of medium-weight string (like a kite string)
- Graph paper
- Straight-edge ruler or yardstick
- Measuring tape
- Scissors
- Pen or marker
- Straight piece of cardboard

STABILITY DETERMINATION

Using graph paper, draw out the top view of your rocket, to scale (1 square = 1 inch), based on the measurements of your rocket. You can also draw a side and bottom view to have a complete record of your rocket's shape and size.

Then carefully place your rocket on the piece of cardboard and trace around it, as closely as you can. Cut out the trace of the rocket.

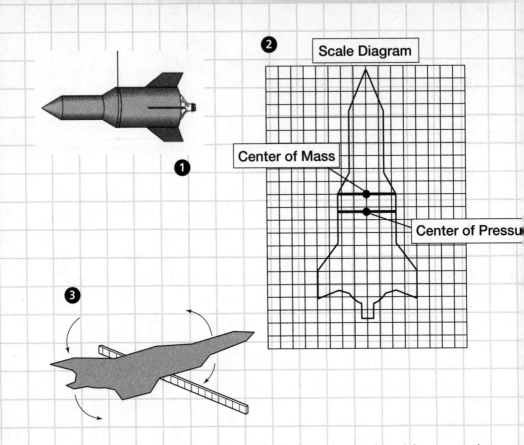

Scale Diagram

Center of Mass

Center of Pressu[re]

Tie a string loop around the middle of your rocket, but keep it loose enough to move along the rocket body as you find the CM for balance. Tie a second string to the first so that you can pick it up. Hold the rocket up in the air and slide the string loop to a position where the rocket balances.

Keeping the string in place, measure how far it is from the nose cone (or bottom) of the rocket. Find the corresponding place on your scale image and mark it with a straight line across the body of the rocket and a dot in the center of the rocket body.

Lay the cardboard silhouette you just cut out on the ruler edge and balance it. Mark the placement of the ruler on your cardboard cutout, then measure and mark your graph paper diagram in the corresponding point. The center is the CP of the rocket.

If your CM is in front of the CP (closer to the nose cone), your rocket should be stable. Proceed to the swing test. If the two centers are next to or on top of each other, add more clay to the nose cone of the rocket. This will move the CM forward. Repeat steps 2 and 3, and then proceed to the swing test.

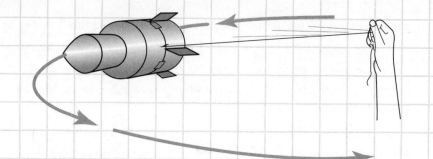

SWING TEST

Tape the string loop you tied around your rocket in the previous set of instructions so that it does not slip.

While standing in an open place, slowly begin swinging your rocket in a circle. If the rocket points in the direction you are swinging it, the rocket is stable. If not, add more clay to the rocket nose cone or replace the rocket fins with larger ones. Repeat the stability determination instructions, and then repeat the swing test.

Once you determine your rocket is stable, securely glue or tape the nose cone in place for launch!

STAGE THREE: CONSTRUCTION OF A ROCKET LAUNCHER

Construct the launcher described below or obtain one from a science or technology-education supply catalog or online store.

Once you have the launcher ready, remember: safety first! Wear properly fitting goggles when launching rockets, and stand back. If you create and launch your rockets in a group, you can create launch safety rules that everybody must follow and roles for each person in the group. Countdowns help everybody to know when the rocket will lift off.

Consult the materials and tools list below to determine what you will need to construct a single bottle rocket launcher. The launcher is inexpensive to construct, but it can also be purchased if you do not have access to the materials needed. We recommend adult assistance in constructing and using the launcher. Because the rockets are projectiles, safely using the launchers will require careful planning and possibly additional supervision. Please refer to the launch safety instructions in the *Adventures in Rocket Science* PDF for more detailed guidance.

Air pressure for the launch is provided by means of a hand-operated bicycle pump. The pump should have a pressure gauge for accurate comparisons between launches. Most needed parts are available from hardware stores. In addition, you will need a tire valve from an auto parts store, and a rubber bottle stopper.

MATERIALS AND TOOLS

- Four 5-inch corner irons with 12.75-inch wood screws to fit
- One 5-inch mounting plate
- Two 6-inch spikes
- Two 10-inch spikes or metal tent stakes
- Two 5-inch-by-0.25-inch carriage bolts with six 0.25-inch nuts
- One 3-inch eyebolt with two nuts and washers
- 0.75-inch diameter washers to fit bolts
- One number 3 rubber bottle stopper with a single hole
- One snap-in tubeless tire valve (small 0.453-inch hole, 2 inches long)
- 12 ×18 × 0.75-inch wood board
- One 2-liter plastic bottle
- Electric drill and bits, including a 0.375-inch bit
- Screwdriver
- Pliers or open-end wrench to fit nuts
- Vise
- 12 feet of 0.25-inch cord
- Pencil
- Bicycle pump with pressure gauge

PROCEDURE

1. Prepare the rubber stopper by enlarging the hole with a drill. Grip the stopper lightly with a vise and gently enlarge the hole with a 0.375-inch bit and electric drill. The rubber will stretch during cutting, making the finished hole somewhat less than 0.375 inch.

2. Remove the stopper from the vise and push the needle valve end of the tire stem through the stopper from the narrow end to the wide end.

3. Prepare the mounting plate by drilling a 0.375-inch hole through the center of the plate. Hold the plate with a vise during drilling and put on eye protection. Enlarge the holes at the opposite ends of the plates,

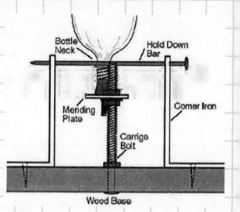

using a drill bit slightly larger than the holes to do this. The holes must be large enough to pass the carriage bolts through them.

4. Lay the mending plate in the center of the wood base and mark the centers of the two outside holes that you enlarged. Drill holes through the wood big enough to pass the carriage bolts through.

5. Push and twist the tire stem into the hole you drilled in the center of the mounting plate. The fat end of the stopper should rest on the plate.

6. Insert the carriage bolts through the wood base from the bottom up. Place a hex nut over each bolt and tighten the nut so that the bolt head pulls into the wood.

7. Screw a second nut over each bolt and spin it about halfway down the bolt. Place a washer over each nut, and then slip the mounting plate over the two bolts.

8. Press the neck of a 2-liter plastic bottle over the stopper. You will be using the bottle's wide neck lip for measuring in the next step.

9. Set up two corner irons so they look like bookends. Insert a spike through the top hole of each iron. Slide the irons near the bottle's neck so that the spike

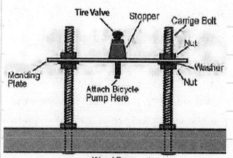

rests immediately above the wide neck lip. The spike will hold the bottle in place while you pump up the rocket. If the bottle is too low, adjust the nuts beneath the mounting plate on both sides to raise it.

10. Set up the other two corner

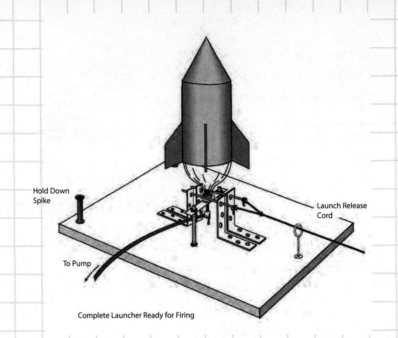

Hold Down Spike

Launch Release Cord

To Pump

Complete Launcher Ready for Firing

irons as you did in the previous step. Place them on the opposite side of the bottle. When you have the irons aligned so that the spikes rest above and hold the bottle lip, mark the centers of the holes on the wood base. For more precise screwing, drill small pilot holes for each screw, and then screw the corner irons tightly to the base.

11. Install an eyebolt to the edge of the opposite holes for the hold-down spikes. Drill a hole, and hold the bolt in place with washers and nuts on top and bottom.

12. Attach the launch pull cord to the head end of each spike. Run the cord through the eyebolt.

13. Make final adjustments to the launcher by attaching the pump to the tire stem and pumping up the bottle. Refer to the launching safety instructions for safety notes. If the air seeps out around the stopper, the stopper is too loose. Use a pair of pliers or a wrench to raise each side of the mounting plate in turn to press the stopper with slightly more force to the bottle's neck. When satisfied with the position, thread the remaining hex nuts over the mounting plate and tighten them to hold the plate in position.

14. Drill two holes through the wood base along one side. The holes should be large enough for large spikes or metal tent stakes to pass through. When the launchpad is set up on a grassy field, the stakes will hold the launcher in place when you yank the pull cord. The launcher is now complete!

216

ALTERNATIVE LAUNCH BASE

QUESTIONS TO INVESTIGATE

▶ *How would a 2-liter bottle fly differently from a half-liter bottle?*
▶ *What if you just put air in the bottle?*
▶ *What happens if I add water to the rocket?*
▶ *How does adding modeling clay to the nose cone affect the rocket's flight?*

As you investigate your new questions, make a hypothesis and then build and launch rockets made from smaller/larger bottles, or change other variables. The straw rocket was launched with just air pressure applied in a pulse. Your bottle rocket can be launched this way but can also employ extra pressure from expelling water. You can increase the force further by adding a small amount of water to the rocket. Adding a small amount of water to the bottle increases the action force. The water expels from the bottle before the air does, turning the bottle rocket into a bigger version of a water rocket toy available in toy stores.

Placing 1.75–3.53 ounces (50–100 grams) of clay into the cone helps to stabilize the rocket by moving the center of mass farther from the center of pressure.

You can explore what relative amounts of air and water propel the rocket better, or make design adjustments to the shape of the fins or nose cone, adding weight or surface area to see how it affects the launch and flight. Observing the flight of various lengths and weights of rockets will add to the inquiry experience.

If you make multiple rockets with a group, have some bottles filled one-fourth, one-third, and one-half full of water.

Pump each rocket with the same amount of air (same number of pumps). Then launch them to see which ones go the highest or farthest.

As you change the design of your rocket to investigate the effect of an individual variable, keep track of your changes and results so you can compare and analyze them.

You can conduct spectacular nighttime launches of your bottle rockets. Make the rockets visible in flight by taping a small-size chemical light stick near the nose cone of each rocket. (Light sticks are available at toy and camping stores and can be used for many flights.)

For more experiments involving rockets, information on Newton's laws of motion, or to learn how you can participate in NASA's rocket design challenge, check out the activities in www.nasa.gov/pdf/265386main_Adventures_In_Rocket_Science.pdf

ACKNOWLEDGMENTS

I t has been said that "the two most important days in your life are the day you were born and the day you find out why."

At thirty-seven years old I was very blessed and thankful for Jeanette Suarez to have had the courage to share with me my "why"—to share my testimony with the world. The conversation actually started with "something is going to happen to you." Those were heavy, almost unbelievable words to hear when I was in the prime of my life, getting ready to reach for the stars. But that five-minute conversation was the driving force behind me writing. There are so many people who've helped guide me on this circuitous fifty-three-year journey, and they kept my path full of positivity, grace, and purpose.

I want to thank my agent, Darnell Strom at Creative Artists Agency, for routinely encouraging me to tell this story. Thanks also to David Larabell for his help in connecting me with the wonderful Tracy Sherrod at Amistad Books and David Linker at HarperCollins Children's Books, who both believed in this project from the start. Many thanks to Simon Sinek for many things but especially for introducing me to Laurie Flynn, who helped get the process started with the proposal. Jabari Asim and Laurie Calkhoven: you helped shape and craft these words, and I appreciate your passion for rich, powerful storytelling.

My family has tirelessly supported me in all my endeavors, no matter how foolish or far out they seemed. Thanks, Mom, Dad, Cat, Allen, Britt, and Ciara. You have always been there for me, and I thank you immensely for your love, encouragement, and support in so many ways. My other family—Louise, Betty, Tom, Chandler, Phyllis, Nanette, Stephanie, Rhonda Ann, Nina, Michael, Branch, Colethia, Cora, Jack, Helen, Anita, Alan, Karen, Harold, Jordon, Renita, Kiera, Geneva, Reggie, Vincent, Arnold, Arnold Jr., Brett, Gregory, Freddie, Rosie, Reen, James, Gladys, Henry, Chante', and others—I thank you. Thanks for neighbors like the Davis, Smith, Kaine, Mabry, Lynch, Jones, Alexander, Brew, Brown, Watson, Fleshman, Bolling, Powell, and Saunders families for getting me back on the straight and narrow when I strayed. Butch, remember you were straying with me.

Perrymont Elementary educators: thanks, Principal

Carwile, for including me in the sixth-grade class you were teaching Algebra to during your break time. That early instruction prepared me for careers in the sciences and in engineering. Educators Sutherland, Bergman, Martin, White, Fowler, Rivers, and others were truly instrumental in my foundational development and I appreciate your dedication and patience. Stan, Kevbo, Duke, Mike, Butch, Stan W., Rophenia, Brandon, J. W., Charade: you were true friends who helped me stay grounded. Educators at Dunbar Middle—Dot Swain, Leah Ingram, Charlie Dawson, Coach Austin, Cobb, Coach Z, and others—kept the poet in me until this day.

Heritage High educators and coaches, I really appreciate you for believing in me. Green, Knight, Storm, Pultz, Gilbert, Farmer, Thomas, Glover, Jones, Hawley, Coleman, Knight, Ratliffe, Patterson, Campbell, Pittas, Davis, Switzer, Clarke, Spencer, Mr. Mark, and others, I thank immensely.

My Jackson Street church family—especially the Williams, Hutcherson, Clarke, Mosely, and other families—I thank you for helping me keep the faith through many times of turmoil and strife. Jerome, Thad, Alvin, and Calvin, I really appreciate you letting me try to hang with the cool college guys.

My University of Richmond football family, I really appreciate all you did to help me develop a strong sense of grit as we overcame so many *L*s on the gridiron.

Coach Shealy, Coach Hout, Coach Shannon, Coach Van Arsdale, T-lack, Bobby B. Hasty, Worrel, "Red Shoes" Gray, roomie Dan Fitz, Napole, Billy Starke, Don Miller, Damon, Gary O., Cal Bell, J. B., Joe "Betty," Jarvis receivers—Jeff, Pup, J. C., John Henry, Doug Ehlers, Johnnie E., and K. J.—were all instrumental in helping me understand what it meant to be on a team, especially during the tough times that first year.

I had a really tough start at the University of Richmond, but there were many people who would not allow me to give up. Dr. Myers (*ad astra*), you and your family have always been there, along with Drs. Clough, Goldman, Bell, and Dominey. I appreciate the lessons that did not pertain just to chemistry but also helped me learn about life. Dr. Heilman, John Roush, and the other leaders who did not give up on Spider football made it possible for my NFL stint and prepared me for setbacks and success in space. You also allowed me to see there was more to UR than what I had experienced early on. I can really appreciate what the university has become and how it creates leaders that make significant contributions to our world.

Thanks, Allyn and Lyle, for being great sounding boards and friends during the Lions' camp.

Thanks to my UVA family for helping me get a graduate degree while trying to play in the NFL and believing that

I could do both. Glenn Stoner, Ray Taylor, George Cahen, Marlene, and B. J., you guys kept the notes coming so that I would not get too far behind. To the Killer Bees, thanks for keeping the summers festive—Peggy M., Norwood, Brian, Rodney, Anita, William W., and A. B. C. at the "diss" house.

My NASA family in Hampton really helped me understand what it meant to be a scientist and engineer and part of a team that wanted to change the world in a positive way through STEM. It was also a family of people who believed in uplifting the marginalized and disenfranchised to help them aspire to do great things.

Thanks to Rudy King, John Simmons, Kendall Freeman, "Big Bill," Sam James, Ted Johnson, Joe Heyman, Thomas Kashangaki, David Shannon, Todd Pilot, Charlie Camarda, Rosa Webster, Woodrow Whitlow, Bob Lee, Katherine Johnson, Glinda Shipman, Joe Heyman, Bill Winfree, Bob Rogowski, Elliot Kramer, Meng Cho-Wu, Brooks Childers, Jason, Mark Froggatt, and many others.

My NASA Johnson family took teamwork to another level, especially when we came together to honor our fallen. All my Penguin classmates, my STS-122 and STS-129 crewmates, I thank you for helping make me a better astro and person. Godspeed to our buddies who have left the planet: STS-107 (Rick, Willie, David, Kalpana, Michael, Laurel, and Ilan), Dex, and Piers. Garrett Reisman, thanks so for much for being a great CACO who kept me laughing even though I could not hear anything you were saying. Shep and G, thanks for an amazing experience in Star City with Kenny, Bob C., Peggy, Julie, Sandy, and the rest of the Russian Crusader bunch. Dennis, Alla, Sergei, Yuri, thank you for inviting me into your homes and sharing your culture, language, and great food with me. The rest of the CB family as well as the training team: you got us ready and supported us in every way to make sure that we were all safe. Erlinda, Beth, and Heather, you controlled my life for ten years and then were there for my family too. Flight Med John Locke and Jon Clark, you fought for me to get back on flight status and I appreciate your efforts. Dr. Rich Williams, I thank you for helping the team get comfortable with me flying in space. Joe Dervay, Smith, Brenda, Amy, C. J., Carole: some of you saw me as an astronaut hopeful and were there to help me get through the labyrinth of forms, documents, and testing to get back on flight status and then get to space; I thank you.

I worked at NASA HQ, which involved two stints that connected me with extremely passionate educators who made a difference in the lives of our most precious resource, our children. Thanks, Charles Scales, for helping me see past my résumé and what could be possible as a different kind of AA for education. The Summer of Innovation crew—Dovie, Carol, Rick, Shelly, Jim, and others—we really helped our kids enjoy STEM over the summer in a hands-on, experiential way. I appreciate all the conferences, symposiums, and gatherings that exposed so many to what we do to share our incredible scientific missions to learners, educators, and the community. As AA, I was really fortunate to work with this incredible team across the agency. Thanks, Education Coordinating Council. Thanks, CoSTEM—especially Joan F. and others for trying to take a coordinated approach to STEM ed. I learned a lot from many of you. Thanks, Carolyn, Roosevelt, Mea, Donald, Carl, Mabel, Mary, Diane, Joeletta, Lenell, and Andrew for keeping me sane.

Friends, family, colleagues, and complete strangers have helped me through this meandering journey thus far: Paris L., Coach Baber, Coach Russel, Jeanette E., Elizabeth, Pharrell, Christian M., Quincy, Beth N. C., Contessa, Curtis, Robert F., Chopper, Jeanette, Doc Alford, Nancy, Jim and Jere S., Yvonne, the Odyssey team, Barrington, Laura R., Dana, Nicole, Annette, Tsipi, Zigi, Gela, Robin, Lisa, Mallory, Hilda, Mrs. Patterson, Barry Barnum, George Ivy, Alan Fred, Fire Station 3, Margot Lee Shetterly, Lani, Rona, Evylynn, Jon, J. P., Sandy, the Brown Family, Karen, Ashley B., Patty O', Sonya D., Olivia, will.i.am, Claudia, Summer, Paul, Ruth, Yolanda, Sherri, Doc Gross, Shaun, Sue, Tom, Willie W., Ed Dwight, Pat S., Leah, and Reggie M. Thanks, Melissa, for taking care of the boys so many times, being a good friend, and helping with the edits. The Star Harbor crew—Maraia, Scott, Ron, Mindy, Jenn, Shubham, Luis, Holly, Robert, Alan, and Bill—thanks for having a vision to make things better on this planet by creating an overview for all to see the possibilities. Thank you, Team Constellation: Guy, Ron, Anousheh, Nicole, Cora, Jeremy, Jacob, and Christoph.

Finally, Charlie Bolden, I thank you for being a great boss and also like a second father to me. You inspired me and so many others to believe and achieve great things.

I really always tried to do the things I enjoyed but did not always connect a purpose to it. All of you have helped me use my "why" to tell this story, and I appreciate your support and love throughout the years.